A BROKEN
BEAUTY

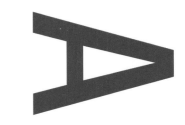

BROKEN
BEAUTY

EDITED BY THEODORE L. PRESCOTT

WILLIAM B. EERDMANS PUBLISHING COMPANY
GRAND RAPIDS, MICHIGAN / CAMBRIDGE, U.K.

Wm. B. Eerdmans Publishing Co.
255 Jefferson Ave. S.E., Grand Rapids, Michigan 49503 /
P.O. Box 163, Cambridge CB3 9PU U.K.

Book design by Kevin van der Leek Design Inc.

Printed in the United States of America

09 08 07 06 05   7 6 5 4 3 2 1

Library of Congress Cataloging-in-Publication Data

A broken beauty / edited by Theodore L. Prescott.
        p.   cm.
   Includes bibliographical references and index.
   ISBN 0-8028-2818-3 (alk. paper)
      1. Human figure in art — Exhibitions. 2. Art and religion — Exhibitions.
   3. Figurative art, American — 20th century — Exhibitions. 4. Figurative art,
   Canadian — 20th century — Exhibitions. I. Prescott, Theodore.

N7570.B76 2005
104.9′42′0904 — dc22

                                          2004065421

www.eerdmans.com

CONTENTS

FOREWORD

One thing that nearly all good stories have in common is that they often begin with a seemingly intractable problem. A forbidden piece of fruit is eaten and paradise is lost. A boy tries to best his father in a flying competition by building a lighter pair of wings; he soars too high, too close to the sun, only to plummet to his death in the sea when his wax wings melt. It seems that this pattern is deeply ingrained in us. We know something is wrong with our world and ourselves, and so we tell our stories in an effort to right it — or at least to honorably set forth the problem. *A Broken Beauty* is predicated upon similar grounds.

My graduate school mentor, Philip Guston,[1] once told a story from his life that helped to galvanize my own sense of purpose as a painter — and it has bearing upon the beginnings of this book and the exhibition it references. Guston had won a *Prix de Rome* and was living in Italy, painting and touring and generally enjoying his good fortune. He had a chance to visit the masterpiece of his hero Piero della Francesca in Arezzo — the mural cycle in Cappella de San Francesco, *The Legend of the True Cross*. When Guston got there with his two friends, he looked up at the magnificent and complex set of images surrounding the little chapel and he wept. When his friends asked him what was wrong, he replied, "We don't have a story. . . . These Christians . . . *they* had a story."

Guston told this to illustrate a point that his late paintings make about life and art, namely that meaning is not to be found in a mania for purity and aesthetic delectation. The culture of epicurean high art that had formed around "pure" abstraction and the New York School in the 1950s had left him with a kind of disgust and enervation, and he wanted us (his students) to understand that great art was deeply indebted to the inheritance of cultural stories. Guston's return to narrative and figurative painting in the late 1960s signaled to a generation that we're not yet done with tradition, nor are we able to rid ourselves of our very human propensity for storytelling.[2]

A Broken Beauty is about this very thing: the rich and problematic nature of beauty and of human experience as it has been given to us via history and the Christian tradition, itself a story or set of stories. We long for completeness and health and perfection; yet more often than not we encounter fragmentation, weakness, and at best a tragicomic dignity like the characters in Guston's late work. In his last paintings there is still an echo of an earlier optimistic belief in the power of art to change society. An example of this would be an early piece entitled *Conspirators* (fig. 1), which shows hooded Klansmen in a cabal of violence and racial injustice. The piece was destroyed by vandals who presumably hated the painting for its voicing of social protest. In a late work, Guston's

---

1. Philip Guston, American (b. 1913, Montreal, Canada; d. 1980, Woodstock, New York). Guston was a prominent New York painter whose work is often grouped with his friends Jackson Pollock and Willem deKooning as part of the Abstract Expressionists — the so-called New York School. Guston, whose works have recently enjoyed a major retrospective at the Metropolitan Museum in New York (Fall-Winter 2003-2004), often mentioned that he felt the "purist" aspirations of many abstractionists were misguided. He is famous for having said, "I got sick and tired of that purity — want to tell Stories" [sic], thus defying the critic Clement Greenberg's dictum that painting should be "pure" — that is, painting about painting, not about literature, history, and other external referents. Guston's late work (ca. 1967-1980) is characterized by cartoon-like style and references to war, social unrest, personal dissipation, and a host of other social, psychological, and political concerns.

Left: Bruce Herman, *Annunciation,* detail (2002)

2. During an interview at the San Francisco Museum of Modern Art, Guston said, "I do not see why a loss of faith in the known image and symbol in our time should be celebrated as a freedom. It is a loss from which we suffer, and this pathos motivated modern painting and poetry at its heart." Guston's return to narrative figuration from his famous "abstract impressionist" period was notorious when he first exhibited the new style of work. One important critic in the *New York Times* called him a "mandarin masquerading as a stumblebum" — referring to the clumsy, cartoon-like figures of his mature phase.

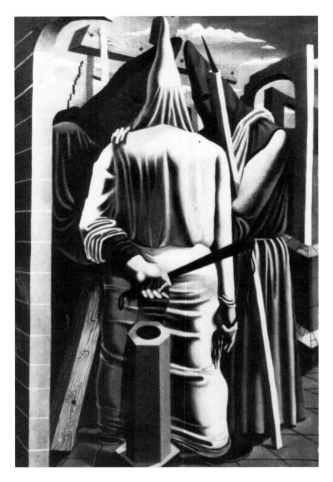

Figure 1. Philip Guston, *Conspirators* (ca. 1930)

outlook is more complex and problematic: the artist is no longer the hero challenging social injustice. In *The Studio* (fig. 2), Guston himself is grouped among the wrongdoers, wearing a hood like the Klansmen. The artist has become, like the late Goya, full of melancholy, harboring a dim view of human nature while still attempting to redeem himself through painting.

The melancholy and brokenness of Guston's late vision has been reflected in the work of many younger artists since 1980. It was in my desire to connect with some of these individuals that I first dreamed up the larger project that brought many of the artists in *A Broken Beauty* together. I was hoping for a conversation that might offer a deeper grasp of the issues surrounding the body, brokenness, and beauty — the preoccupations of nearly three decades of my art — and regarding similar issues raised by the darker feelings let loose in the late Guston.

Due to the generosity and prompting of Patricia Jones, a patron and friend, I began writing a series of essays and proposals that invited a small group of artists, patrons, and interpreters to collaborate on an exhibit of works referencing these themes — particularly the theme of brokenness and how it often occasions a unique beauty characterized as much by moral insight as by purist aesthetic considerations.

My thought was that by inviting a diverse group of artists to help shape the proposed exhibition, a common set of themes and images might emerge in the midst of the inevitable differences. My own conviction is that, despite cultural and historical differences in the human family, there exists a common set of stories that play themselves out in all tribes and all times. My earnest hope was that these common threads might point us toward a certain visual and theoretical unity in the proposed exhibit.

This initial aim has been more than met, and the expansion of the original exhibition concept into the current book and touring show is much like any good conversation; it takes unexpected turns and twists and in the end is better for it. After the initial discussions at the first meeting, David Goa, Emeritus Curator at the Provincial Museum of Alberta in Edmonton, met with art historian Gordon Fuglie,

who is Director of the Laband Art Gallery at Loyola
Marymount University in Los Angeles. The two
developed the conceptual framework of the exhibition in 2002, setting in place the thematic foci of the
project. Working in concert, they met and discussed
the themes that later became the core of both the
exhibition and this book — offering such rubrics as
After the Fall, Presence Encountered, Sanctified, and
Terrors of History, among others.

The thoughtful examination of the artists' works
by Goa and Fuglie and the search for categories
and thematic material yielded insight both into
the works in the *Broken Beauty* exhibit and into a
dominant issue in the art world today: the recovery
of beauty[3] as a primary concern of visual art. Each of
the essays contained in this volume references the
problematic status of beauty and the human image
in some way, attempting to relate the works of *A Broken Beauty* to this larger conversation — either from
the standpoint of the broader Western tradition or
by examining the current art world context for critical appraisal of issues specific to this group of artists.

Every era witnesses the contest of various voices
for the telling of a culture's story, and most Modernist voices told a story that seemed to eclipse the
possibility of the human presence as a meaningful
image in a time of massive cultural change. Theodore
Prescott, Distinguished Professor of Art at Messiah
College and the editor of *A Broken Beauty,* wrote
"The Bodies Before Us." This chapter shows how the
human presence was never really abandoned in
modernity — and in fact that the apparent rejection
of beauty and the body have been more the result of
the selective eye of influential critics and historians
than an actual diminution of the humanist tradition
in art. Prescott examines problems in the perception
of religion in contemporary art and asks how artists
of the last quarter century have tended to look at the
figure. He examines the work of four contemporary

Figure 2. Philip Guston, *The Studio* **(ca. 1969)**

3. Cf. Gordon Fuglie's essay in the current volume, "Beauty Lost,
Beauty Found: One Hundred Years of Attitudes," along with Theodore
Prescott's "The Bodies Before Us." These essays help to scope out the
terrain of current art theory and describe for the general reader how
the two — art and beauty — came to be sundered in the modern era.

artists for what he calls influential art world attitudes about the human image. He ends the essay with a reflection on some Christian concepts of embodiment that embrace both beauty and brokenness.

Timothy Verdon, who is an art historian and director of the Museo del Opera del Duomo in Florence, Italy, explores Southern (largely Roman Catholic) European tradition of the human form in "Broken Beauty, Shattered Heart." The art he discusses is clearly indebted to the Christian theological proposition that the physical body is good (as contrasted with the gnostic notion that we must transcend the dross of the physical in order to attain the perfection of a non-physical consciousness). Verdon also touches upon the profound anomy and fragmentation that characterized much of Modernist art in the wake of a century of horrific wars (a consequence of which was the widespread dehumanization of art and rejection of beauty as a worthy aim in the face of such horror).

Lisa J. DeBoer, an art historian at Westmont College in Santa Barbara, explores another strand of tradition that has shaped the consciousness of figurative artists in the past four centuries — the "comic" vision of the human form in Northern European painting. Her chapter "A Comic Vision? Northern Renaissance Art and the Human Figure" reveals how Protestant theology, with its vision of the smallness, weakness, and brokenness of humanity in the face of the vastness of Nature, contributed a different view of the body from the heroic vision of the South. DeBoer connects the Northern school with the Southern via Dante's *Divina Comedia,* elucidating the influence of a deeply Christian vision of hope and ultimate glory hidden in the humiliation of earthly flesh and ordinariness. Her essay ends with a consideration of whether or not the tradition of the comic-tragic human story has further possibilities for contemporary art.

Gordon Fuglie, Curator of the *Broken Beauty* exhibition, also challenges the influential voices of the current art world in his first essay, "Beauty Lost, Beauty Found: One Hundred Years of Attitudes," in which he explores the resurgence of figurative painting in the past thirty years. Fuglie decries the prevailing prejudices in TAW (an acronym for "The Art World" coined

by Doug Harvey) against intended religious imagery, along with the insularity of TAW's shrinking *coterie.* He then describes one view of beauty that was influential in modern art at mid-century. That view was articulated by the Neo-Thomist philosopher Jacques Maritain — who knew and respected the artists of his time — and was shared within a secular understanding by the American art historian Meyer Schapiro. Fuglie's second essay, "*A Broken Beauty* and Its Artists," situates the artists represented in *A Broken Beauty* within a broad context of the postmodern reclamation of the figurative tradition; he sets forth the structure of the exhibit and its thematic foci, showing how a biblical worldview supplies the subtext of the artists' works and the traditions they reference.

The art work and the artists reflected in this volume — both the group of fifteen contemporary artists featured here and their predecessors, Piero, Giotto, Rembrandt, Van Eyk, and the host of other great artists referenced in the following essays — have all sought to bear witness to the surprising beauty found in moments of suffering or loss or brokenness. Unlike the potential hubris of a more purist aesthetic, *A Broken Beauty* strives to show the mystery and mess of a *story* that is far from over — one that is ever more complex and problematic, yet moving toward a sense of resolution. Like the Bible, itself a tragicomic story that begins with a cosmic problem and ends in a wedding feast, *A Broken Beauty* suggests possible ways out of the angst-ridden *miserific* vision toward a recovery of the *beatific* vision of hope — something that is badly needed in our troubled times.

It is a privilege and an honor to contribute some small part to this vision of hopeful humanity and to participate in the continuance of the great cultural conversation that underwrites it. It is my conviction that posterity depends on this hope being renewed in our day. It is our prayer that *A Broken Beauty* is a small step toward this renewal.

BRUCE HERMAN
Professor of Art and Chair of the Art Department
Gordon College
Wenham, Massachusetts

ACKNOWLEDGMENTS

This project, both the exhibition and the book *A Broken Beauty,* would not have been possible without the help and support of many. We would like to thank Patricia Jones for her initiative in seeking out artist Bruce Herman in the first place and prompting him to dream a bit about a possible public exhibit of contemporary artists whose works reference the sacred art traditions — and for her unstinting help and financial support from the beginning. We would also like to acknowledge the financial support of the Ahmanson Charitable Community Trust and the Coalition for Christian Colleges and Universities for their generous support. We thank Gordon College, particularly Craig Hammon, former Vice President, and Mark Sargent, Provost, for providing an institutional home for the project, and David Goss, Adjunct Professor of History, for his tireless clerical assistance and public relations work early on.

For help in structuring the exhibition and for much of the conceptual groundwork and educational outreach we would like to thank David Goa, Emeritus Curator of the Provincial Museum of Alberta, Canada, and Gordon Fuglie, Director of Laband Art Gallery at Loyola Marymount University in Los Angeles.

We would like to acknowledge the initial exhibition venues, the Laguna Art Museum of Laguna Beach, California; and the Joseph D. Carrier Gallery of Toronto, Canada. Numerous individuals and organizations in these cities have offered financial and volunteer help in the realization of exhibition events. For all of these we are profoundly grateful, and thanks especially to John Franklin, Director of IMAGO (Toronto), for his help in fundraising and organizing events for the exhibition in Canada.

We thank Sandra DeGroot, Project Developer at William B. Eerdmans Publishing, for her patient and supportive work coordinating the complex set of issues surrounding the book and its authors. For help in the many administrative aspects of both the book and the exhibition, and for indexing the book, we owe a debt of love to Michelle Arnold, of Gordon College. Many thanks also to Jean McCauslin, secretary for the Department of Art at Messiah College, and Seleena Lindsey, publishing technician in Messiah's Faculty Services Office, for their capable, cheerful work under short deadlines. We also need to acknowledge the beautiful design work for the website of *A Broken Beauty* completed by Timothy Ferguson-Sauder and his staff at the Return Design Collaborative (Gordon College) and for the handsome book design by Kevin van der Leek Design Inc., of Vancouver, BC.

Lastly we must acknowledge the artists and authors of *A Broken Beauty* whose works grace these pages, and the extraordinary patience and care exercised by the editor of this volume, Ted Prescott.

The contributors to *A Broken Beauty*

THE BODIES BEFORE US

Theodore L. Prescott

A *Broken Beauty* is an exhibition of works by fifteen North American artists who depict the human image. In some of the works there are clear references to biblical or Christian subjects, while in others there is no overt religious content. The artist who conceived the exhibition, Bruce Herman, has the ambitious goal of wanting to call attention to contemporary artists who have some debt to historic understanding of the human image. That understanding, grounded in the intertwining of Western Classical and Christian traditions, unites experiences we often keep separate, such as joy and suffering, wholeness and loss, beauty and ugliness, or the capacity for hope when faced with overwhelming evil. Quite simply, Herman wants to raise questions about the human imagery of our times.

It is commonplace to describe our culture as visually saturated. Certainly the average North American is awash in a deluge of pictures: blissful consumers; surreally beautiful models; live video reports of indescribable atrocities; and "entertainment" that depends on more and more spectacular forms of destruction and dismemberment. While we often complain about mass media, we understand its uses and generally assume that we know what the images in mass media represent.

When it comes to art, students and friends have asked me over the years why so many of the pictures of people in the modern period seem disturbing. Why have artists chosen to depict people the way they have? Sometimes the questions are about liberties artists take with the human form. With these questions the syntax of the photograph may hover silently in the background as the preferred standard for reality. But sometimes the distortions of the human form seem to be made for psychological or spiritual

Left: Richard Harden, *My Breath,* detail (2001)

reasons and to convey a sense of deep unease, or malaise. Though the boundaries between the "high" and popular arts have eroded in the last quarter century, people still look at the art in galleries and museums as charged with meaning. Thus questions about how people are represented, and what disturbing pictures might mean, are no surprise.

In the following essay I will address the perception of the human image in North American visual art. It is a complex topic, so my foray is necessarily selective and limited. I begin with a description of an exhibition, *New Images of Man,* which has some significant parallels to *A Broken Beauty*. Since both exhibitions have acknowledged the religious dimensions of human experience, I describe some of the problems religious imagery poses for audiences and artists in contemporary art. Following this, I discuss the work of four well-known artists who are not a part of the *Broken Beauty* project. I believe they represent popular and influential ways people are pictured and understood within art's culture. Finally, after a brief consideration of contemporary Classical imagery, I conclude with a meditation on a Christian understanding of human embodiment.

The *New Images of Man* Exhibition

In 1959 the Museum of Modern Art mounted an exhibition titled *New Images of Man*. The show was organized by Peter Selz, the curator of painting and sculpture at the museum. It included multiple works by twenty-three European and American artists who had depicted the human figure in the preceding decade. *New Images* was stylistically diverse, mixing work like the thin, attenuated figures of Alberto Giacometti (fig. 1) with the lush but lonely canvases of San Francisco Bay painters Richard Diebenkorn

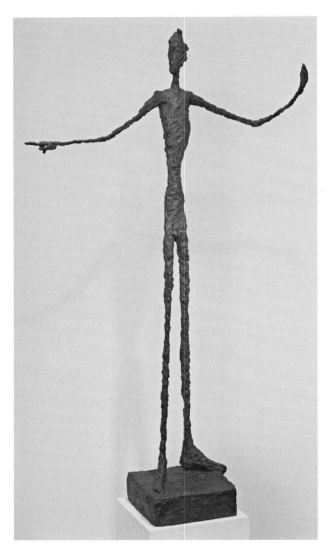

Figure 1. Alberto Giacometti, *Man Pointing* (1947)

and Nathan Olivera. People usually associated with abstraction like Jackson Pollock were included, as were artists whose orientation was primitivist and expressionistic, such as the Chicagoan Leon Golub. He was one of the original members of the "monster roster," a name given to a group of postwar Chicago artists whose work was raw and confrontational. Other artists in the exhibit whose work continues to be esteemed today include Francis Bacon, Willem de Kooning, Jean Dubuffet, and H. C. Westerman.

One way to understand the "New" of the title is in relation to the dominance of abstract art in America during the late 1940s and much of the 1950s. The wide critical success and public notoriety of New York abstract artists, which had been fueled by some intensely partisan cheerleading, gave the impression that figurative and representational art had virtually ceased to exist in postwar America. Nothing could be further from the truth, but it is an easily held misperception. In addition to critical narrowness, this perception was underwritten by an idea of history and style that was progressive and successive. Thus for many partisans — the critic Clement Greenberg, who tirelessly promoted artists like Jackson Pollock, is the obvious example — abstraction rightfully *replaced* an older, no longer tenable art based on figurative imagery.

The critic Robert Hughes described the problems with this view in an introduction to a book about American figurative painters that was published almost twenty-five years after the *New Images* exhibition, when the notion of a figurative return was once again being discussed in the circles of advanced art.

> The truth, of course, is that realist painting in America did not hibernate in the 50s, and was not woken in the 80s. Instead, people stopped looking at it because they felt they ought only, or mainly, to be looking at abstract art or Pop. The art world thought realism was old-fashioned; to cover its mistake it now talks about revivals. It believed that, whatever happened among the eddies and reeds at its edges, the mainstream of modern art flowed toward reduction, to abstraction. . . . Images of the real world were approved to the extent

that they could be treated as signs, demonstrations of linguistic interplay and irony, as in Pop; but in general, the dogma was that only abstraction contained higher seriousness and pointed to the future.[1]

The "New" in the *New Images* exhibition can also be understood in another way. Many exponents of modern art believed that our cultural, social, and moral circumstances were fundamentally changed by the crisis of modernity. Thus the old, received ideas and images could no longer speak to the exigencies of our times, and *new* images would have to be found. This kind of thinking is evident in Wassily Kandinsky's famous 1912 *On the Spiritual in Art,* which argued for the appropriateness of abstraction as an antidote to the materialism of the times. In his introduction to the *New Images* catalog Peter Selz wrote,

> The revelations and complexities of mid-twentieth century life have called forth a profound feeling of solitude and anxiety. The imagery of man which has evolved from this reveals sometimes a new dignity, sometimes despair, but always the uniqueness of man as he confronts his fate. Like Kierkegaard, Heidegger, Camus, these artists are aware of anguish and dread, of life in which man — precarious and vulnerable — confronts the precipice, is aware of dying as well as living.[2]

Later in the introduction Selz cites the recent experiences of Buchenwald and Hiroshima and the possibility of nuclear annihilation or technological dehumanization as the social and psychic ground for the artists' work.[3] It is no doubt this perception of the age as unsettled, threatened, and facing existential dread that gave the diverse *New Image* artists a commonality. There were no sun-dappled nudes, no wholesome human relationships, no confident Classical bodies — the misshapen, deformed, or eviscerated figure was the common artistic denominator.

The *New Images of Man* catalog not only raised the question of what was the appropriate human image for the modern postwar age, but it also cast the question in faintly religious terms, since the theologian Paul Tillich wrote a short prefatory essay for it. Tillich was the only mid-century Protestant theologian of any stature to engage art seriously, and indeed the role of art in culture was central to his thinking. (It should be noted that the Catholic Neo-Thomist philosophers Jacques Maritain and Etienne Gilson had both written and lectured about art in the United States. In France there was a short but influential sacred arts movement after World War II, led by Father Couturier, who sought to bring the best contemporary artists into the Catholic church and arranged commissions for Fernand Leger, Marc Chagall, Georges Rouault, and Germaine Richier, among others. Richier was also in the *New Images* show.)[4]

Tillich's experiences of trench warfare in World War I shattered his optimism about human existence. He felt he had experienced "the actual death of this time" and came to believe that "life itself is not dependable ground."[5] On his last furlough he visited the Kaiser Freidrich Museum in Berlin and had a transformative moment in front of Botticelli's *Madonna with Singing Angels.* He felt "a state approaching ecstasy. In the beauty of the painting was Beauty itself. . . . As I stood there bathed in the beauty its painter had envisioned so long ago, something of the divine source of all things came through to me. . . . That moment has affected my whole life, given me the keys for the interpretation of human existence, brought vital joy and spiritual truth."[6]

Art became important for Tillich's theology and

---

1. "Foreword" by Robert Hughes, in *Art of the Real: Nine American Figurative Painters,* ed. Mark Strand (New York: Clarkson Potter/Crown, 1983), p. 7.

2. Peter Selz, *New Images of Man* (New York: Museum of Modern Art/Arno Press, 1969), p. 11.

3. Selz, *New Images of Man,* p. 12.

4. Maritain delivered the first of the prestigious A. W. Mellon Lectures in the Fine Arts at the National Gallery of Art in Washington, D.C., in 1952; his lecture was published as *Creative Intuition in Art and Poetry.* Gilson's *Painting and Reality* was the fourth lecture, given in 1955. The sacred art movement is described in *Modern Sacred Art and the Church of Assy* by William Rubin, who was the chief curator at the Museum of Modern Art for many years.

5. Wolfgang Pauck and Marion Pauck, *Paul Tillich: His Life and Thought,* vol. 1 (New York: Harper & Row, 1976), p. 51.

6. John Dillenberger and Jane Dillenberger, eds., *Paul Tillich on Art and Architecture* (New York: Crossroad, 1987), p. xix.

philosophy. Aesthetically he gravitated toward an "expressionism" that was influenced by progressive artistic movements in Germany during the first quarter of the twentieth century. He distinguished superficial realism from expressive art. For Tillich the former is concerned with the depiction of the visible world, while the latter expresses the depth of human experience through forms and subjects that are shaped by inner, spiritual realities. Tillich saw this expressionism manifested in diverse styles and cultures, and he spoke appreciatively of the Byzantine, Gothic, and Baroque periods. He argued that there was more genuine religious content in paintings of common subjects by Van Gogh than in pictures of conventional religious subjects made by popular late-nineteenth-century painters.[7]

Tillich was a good choice to lend his considerable reputation to the *New Images* exhibition. If the premise of the exhibition was that the contemporary period was unique in the horrors it had witnessed and the threats it faced, which in turn required a new imagery for the human situation, Tillich offered a rough theological and cultural parallel to that idea. His theology was shaped by events on the world stage and by his own personal struggles, which led him to develop a view of religion that he believed suited the current world. An important element of his thought was that religion needed to be reinterpreted in light of contemporary culture, that what was eternal and unchanging was ultimately unable to be expressed or represented in a fixed, transcultural way.[8] Thus the authentically religious could be encountered within the depths of human experience, but it was not necessarily mediated by conventional religious categories or symbols.

It seems fair to say that in Tillich's theology, as in his view of art, he often found the authentic existing outside of received or traditional categories. This

raises interesting questions regarding how we know that something is authentic and whether it is really possible to communicate outside of conventions. Certainly the history of art would show that expressionism quickly fell into stylistic conventions, even if its aim was to operate outside of them. Perhaps religion, too, requires conventions to communicate beliefs.

Critically, *New Images* was a controversial exhibit. Some of the most hostile reviews reproached the museum and Selz for daring to exhibit figurative work during the period when American *abstract* art had supposedly ascended triumphant over the European Modernists — particularly the French "School of Paris."[9] Other reactions centered around whether such disturbing, alienated, absurd, or mutilated bodies were really *the* human image for the time. Several critics pointed out that earlier periods had some disturbing images too. Since most of the artists in the exhibit were well known before the exhibition, some critics argued that the concept of the imagery being new was misleading.[10]

Fairfield Porter, a critic and realist painter whose subjects were his family, friends, and immediate environs, wrote in *The Nation*,

> The violent image of man has the purpose of making a creation acceptable to critics, . . . for these paintings and sculptures seem to mean something profound in proportion to the amount of their distortion and the violence of their appearance, . . . and in this way the artist clears himself from a conscience made uneasy by his choice to be only an artist in a society where moral threats emanate from sociologists and popular threats from politicians.[11]

---

7. Dillenberger and Dillenberger, *Paul Tillich on Art and Architecture,* p. 69.

8. Michael Palmer, *Paul Tillich's Philosophy of Art* (Berlin: Walter De Gruyter, 1984). The entire book is devoted to an unfolding of Tillich's view on art. In describing Tillich's desire to eradicate the distinction between culture and religion, Palmer says, "Tillich's solution lies in his redefinition of religion" (p. 35).

9. Peter Selz, *Beyond the Mainstream: Essays on Modern and Contemporary Art* (New York: Cambridge University Press, 1998), p. 6. I am grateful to Gordon Fuglie for bringing this passage to my attention.

10. Both Katherine Kuh in the *Saturday Review,* October 24, 1959, and Ailene B. Saarinen in the *New York Times Sunday Magazine,* September 27, 1959, discussed earlier precedents. Even Selz in his catalog essay connected *New Images* to some previous works of art.

11. Porter Fairfield, "Art," *The Nation,* October 17, 1959, pp. 240-41.

New Images and *A Broken Beauty*

We can note three aspects of the *New Images* exhibition that *A Broken Beauty* shares or parallels in some way. First, *New Images* was an early manifestation of an artistic and critical interest in possible meanings of the human image during the last half of the twentieth century. In the period since *New Images* that interest has grown considerably but has been diversely expressed. Artists have pictured, deployed, or investigated the human body with differing intentions and critical receptions. Such heterogeneity may suggest a lack of cultural stability regarding an understanding of humanness. That instability has also been seen in the political and philosophic polemics of the "culture wars." Many of our most contentious cultural debates — abortion, human sexuality, euthanasia, the power of the state to coerce individual behavior — are about what can be done to and with the human body.

Second, as evidenced by the critical reactions to the exhibition, *New Images* raised the issue of how beauty and ugliness are seen in the human form, and what those perceptions indicate about our collective hopes and fears. The reactions to *New Images* seemed to suggest that most people didn't think the times merited such disturbing art; but why indeed are beauty and ugliness so meaningfully charged, and why had modern art reacted against the long Western tradition of figural beauty? By the time of the *New Images* show in 1959, the Classical figurative tradition, which had been a major locus of cultural ideas about beauty, had been moribund for close to a century. At least that's the account canonical studies of Modernism like John Canaday's *Mainstreams of Modern Art* (1959) or H. H. Arnason's *Encyclopedia of Modern Art* (1977) gave in their historical surveys.[12]

Clearly the Classical tradition declined over time. At some point, its "death" could be seen in the works of artists who represented modernity. No single artist administered the last rites for the tradition. But certainly Picasso with his *Les Demoiselles d'Avignon* (fig. 2) of 1907 might be seen to officiate at the funeral, given that the vestiges of the Classical subject *The Three Graces* on the left is overwhelmed by a cubist syntax, by widely discussed ethno-graphic appropriations, and by subject matter — a brothel — that debases "old" ideas of grace and virtue.[13]

Finally, the religious element of the *New Images* show, found in the interpretive presence of Paul Tillich, was significant because religion in general and Christianity in particular had only marginal presence in the development of modern art. While there was interest on the part of theologically oriented people like Tillich and Maritain in modern art, modern artists themselves seldom brought religious commitment or a sustained interest in religious subjects into the body of their work. The development of modern art can be used to illustrate the secularization thesis that was popular with some twentieth-century sociologists. That theory held that religion withered away in the face of modern knowledge and consciousness.

Thus Georges Rouault, the Frenchman whose Christian commitment stands out within the canon of modern art, is one of a small minority of religiously oriented artists. The German Emil Nolde and the Russian Jewish artist Marc Chagall are two other modern artists with visible religious interests. But any account of religion in modern art is brief, and its history shows far fewer religious subjects than earlier periods in Western art.[14]

One way in which religious sentiments have

12. John Canaday, *Mainstreams of Modern Art* (New York: Holt, Rinehart and Winston, 1959), and H. H. Arnason, *History of Modern Art,* 2nd ed. (Englewood Cliffs: Prentice-Hall; New York: Harry N. Abrams, 1977). Both authors describe the ascendancy of modern art in relation to the decline of the French Academy, which sought to uphold the Classical tradition.

13. It is interesting to note that Picasso periodically returned to Classical subjects and forms, which belies the idea of a linear stylistic progression dear to champions of Modernism.

14. During the nineteenth century, the first full century of modernity, there were still many religious commissions and religious subjects made throughout the century. Some indication of this can be seen in *Christian Imagery in French 19th Century Art* (Shepherd Gallery Associates, 1980), an exhibition catalog that surveys Christian art made in France between 1789 and 1906. One reason why religious art has had less visibility is that progressive artists and critics, who championed modernity, disparaged religious art, which was often stylistically conservative. Michael Paul Driskel's *Representing Belief* (University Park: Pennsylvania State University Press, 1992) is an excellent study of the history of the conflict between progressive and conservative styles (and beliefs) in nineteenth-century France.

Figure 2. Pablo Picasso, *Les Demoiselles d'Avignon* **(1907)**

continued in modern art is through individuals and movements that have professed *spiritual* aspirations. We can see artists turning toward spirituality in the nineteenth century, but the connections between spirituality and art developed more fully in the last century with artists like Wassily Kandinsky.[15] He saw abstraction as a way to point toward a hidden, spiritual reality that transcends our material world. There has been a strong relationship between concepts of the spiritual and abstraction since then, though the word "spiritual" is now used more generally.[16] By the end of the twentieth century, it was not unusual to hear many kinds of art spoken of in terms of their spiritual qualities.

What distinguishes spirituality from religion is its individual and personal orientation. Spirituality tends to resist creedal or catechetical formulations and to favor individual experience. While those that think in terms of spirituality often draw on the teachings of traditional religions, they do not feel bound by them.[17] Religious institutions, with their very checkered histories, codified practices and beliefs, and bureaucratic structures, are often seen as impediments to the spirit. Spirituality is personally determined and open-ended, while religion has been seen as closed, corporate, hierarchical, and dogmatic.

The Perception and Interpretation of Religion in Contemporary Art

It is important to acknowledge the critical and perceptual thickets surrounding religion in modern and contemporary art. It is not simply that conventional

15. See Wassily Kandinsky, *Concerning the Spiritual in Art,* trans. M. T. H. Sadler (New York: Dover, 1977).

16. Robert Rosenblum's *Modern Painting and the Northern Romantic Tradition* (New York: Harper & Row, 1975) traces the development of spirituality in art and shows its relationship to older Christian iconography. *The Spiritual in Art: Abstract Painting 1890-1985,* ed. Edward Weisberger (New York: Abbeville Press and the Los Angeles County Museum of Art, 1986), is the catalog of a large exhibition of painting with spiritual content.

17. In *Creative Spirituality: The Way of the Artist* (Berkeley: University of California Press, 2001), sociologist Robert Wuthnow notes, "To a striking degree, contemporary artists speak more comfortably about spirituality than about organized religion" (p. 7).

religious subjects have been largely absent from modern art, so that religiously inclined viewers, like Paul Tillich, might need to adjust their definition of what counts as a religious subject. Since the 1980s we have seen a small flurry of religious subjects, even if they sometimes seem designed to make conventionally religious people uncomfortable. Rather, what is problematic is that religion raises questions of interpretation.

North American culture rightly celebrates its diversity and pluralism. There is no religious or artistic orthodoxy, and the art community in particular is boisterously assertive of the rights of *individual* expression. The individuals that speak about the meanings of art include the artists who make the work, the public who sees it, and the critics, curators, and historians who are professional interpreters and act as cultural gatekeepers regarding importance and significance.

Usually critics don't indicate what they think regarding religious belief, but Arthur Danto, the widely respected art critic for *The Nation,* made his opinion pretty clear when he wrote about the abstract paintings of Mark Rothko. He was addressing the beauty in Rothko's art, but he felt it necessary to disengage beauty from its long association with the Divine, which is the way many artists and viewers in the nineteenth century would have been predisposed to understand beauty. He wrote,

> Under Hudson River School metaphysics, natural and artistic beauty were entirely of a piece, as Kant had believed. Their landscapes delivered the kinds of meaning nature itself did when it was beautiful. *One main difference between those painters and ourselves is that we cannot believe in transcendent beings who address humanity through the media of volcanoes and cascades.* So for just that reason, a painting today, done as realistically as a Hudson River School landscape, could not convey to us the meanings Kant believed natural beauty was designed to transmit.[18]

18. Arthur Danto, "Rothko and Beauty," in *The Madonna of the Future: Essays in a Pluralistic Art World* (Berkeley: University of California Press, 2001), p. 337; emphasis added.

Religious beliefs may be acceptable as historical residue, but for Danto it is evidently unthinkable that people would continue to see nature as religiously expressive today.

In *Pictures and Tears,* a recent book that investigates the phenomena of weeping as a response to paintings, art historian James Elkins takes issue with the idea that modern art is without religion. He believes that religious sentiments are a continuing presence in people's engagement of art. Elkins knows that crying in front of art is at odds with the distanced, dry intellectual discourse about art that he identifies as typical of twentieth-century historians and critics. He begins and ends his book with accounts of people's responses to the fourteen somber Mark Rothko abstractions in an interdenominational chapel in Houston. Elkins thinks "it is likely that the majority of people who have wept over twentieth century paintings have done so in front of Rothko paintings."[19] While there are many reasons people cry over paintings, including the fact that they don't know *why* they cry, Elkins suspects that one reason is related to religion, and he details the long history of pictures used to provoke religious empathy. But this is difficult to discuss in today's critical climate. Toward the end of the book, speaking of two different views about the art of our times, he says, "in my experience even the most stringent and theoretically informed post modern painting is suffused with a lingering nostalgia for a time when religion could be named, and tears could be believed, but I can't prove it because the subject — even in this age of apparent freedom of speech — is proscribed."[20] Later Elkins says, "There are writers, more prudent than I am, who don't even broach theology when it comes to art. Religion seeps through everything that's written about modern art, but it's the thought that dare not speak its name."[21]

Another problem raised by religion is the associa-

19. James Elkins, *Pictures and Tears: A History of People Who Have Cried in Front of Paintings* (New York: Routledge, 2001), p. 4. I am indebted to Lisa DeBoer for directing me to Elkins's discussion of religion.
20. Elkins, *Pictures and Tears,* p. 201.
21. Elkins, *Pictures and Tears,* p. 214.

Figure 3. Howard Finster, *The Way of Jesus* (1982)

tive baggage that religion and religious words carry. For example, during the controversies surrounding Andres Serrano's *Piss Christ* (a photograph of a plastic crucifix submerged in urine) in the early 1990s, many Christians were vociferous in their outrage. The defenders of Serrano sometimes labeled these religious critics "puritanical" or "puritans." This designation apparently explained how and why the criticisms were narrow and intolerant. Interestingly, art historian Sally Promey has contrasted the actual practices of Puritans — who in sermons occasionally compared spiritual conversion to sexual orgasm — with the stereotypes of Puritans in American popular culture. Her point is that such stereotyping is not only misinformed but also prejudicial to meaningful exchange, as it "oversimplifies the variety of cultural and political investments represented in this public debate."[22]

There has not been much examination of how beliefs affect our perceptions of art, though responses to both artworks and critical debates must surely be influenced by them. Authors Tim Van Laar and Leonard Diepeveen are the only people I am aware of to have directly addressed the role of belief in and around art. In *Active Sights* they characterize the clash between differing beliefs about art as "inelegant conflict," and they point out that the artists' beliefs about what they are doing may be at odds with the public or critical reception of the artists' work. They note that Howard Finster, the Southern rural preacher turned artist, whose quirky, evangelistically motivated works were enthusiastically embraced by art world cognoscenti, is an example of someone whose "idiosyncratic beliefs can become a way of enhancing a reputation even as they are seriously misunderstood."[23] (See fig. 3.)

Finster saw his art as a kind of visual preaching, but his popularity in the art world was surely enhanced by artistic stereotypes. Finster fulfilled the role of the "primitive," which has fascinated

22. Sally Promey, "The 'Return' of Religion in the Scholarship of American Art," *The Art Bulletin* 85, no. 3 (September 2003): 598.
23. Leonard Diepeveen and Tim Van Laar, *Active Sights: Art as Social Interaction* (Mountain View, CA: Mayfield Publishing, 1998), p. 47.

progressive artists and their audiences since the late nineteenth century. The self-taught, visionary Finster was raw and "naive," and he came from rural Georgia, far outside of our centers of cultural sophistication.

"Attitudes" in Contemporary Art

In subsequent chapters in this volume, Timothy Verdon and Lisa DeBoer have written of the beliefs that animated artists' work across the centuries and provided a *vision* of what it meant to be human. One can only speak of "visions" today, and even that cautious pluralism must be qualified. We see the overwhelming majority of human images today in mass media as entertainment, commerce, or news. Even for a highly successful artist, the audience provided by the museum, the gallery, the art journal, or the book is minuscule compared to, say, the audience for *Friends* or *Law and Order* on any given evening. The images found in the art world, even those that utilize the technology of mass media, are rarified. Then too, to speak of visions the way Verdon and DeBoer do is to depict an enterprise that is wholistic, essentially shared by the larger culture, and stretches across time with continuity, history, and layered depth. For all of its complexity, the art of our time seems cut off from this larger sense of vision. Thus it is more accurate to speak of *attitudes* that are implicit or explicit in our art than to talk about a full-orbed *vision*.

These qualifications must be kept in mind as we turn to look at human and bodily imagery in the art world. In the following pages I describe the work of four contemporary artists who exemplify some influential approaches to the human image. I have chosen these well-known artists because of their wide exposure and the extensive critical discussion that surrounds their work. It seems to me that the ideas associated with these artists' work represent common attitudes (or beliefs) about the human condition within influential circles of the art community. I have taken pains to quote from both artists

and critics to give as full a picture as possible about how meanings are formed. It is interesting to note that sometimes artists don't agree with the critical interpretations of their work; but for those that care about art's meanings, the critic or historian is often seen as more authoritative than the artist.[24] It is my contention that the attitudes I describe are indicative of the artistic environment out of which *A Broken Beauty* emerges.

Four Influential Contemporary Artists

The painter **Philip Pearlstein**, who is now over eighty years old, was one of the first artists to choose to work with the figure over and against the dominant abstract-expressionism of the 1950s. His early work was deeply influenced by the thick, brushy, gesturally expressive painting of the New York School. But by the early 1960s his work had evolved and matured into paintings that are dryly executed, closely cropped, and abstractly composed from studio poses of one or two models. (See fig. 4.) Pearlstein has been very influential both through his work and through his written statements about his goals and practices.

Some of what Pearlstein was doing was *reacting* to artistic ideas that had hardened into dogma. Writing in 1977, he stated that he wanted to get rid of a literary content which he identified as liberal middle-class existentialism, with its expressive paint handling and suggestions of angst and doubt.[25] (Think *New Images*.) In doing this, Pearlstein was

24. It is important to point out that by looking only at the possible meaning of an artist's work we distort the experience of art. We can reduce art to a series of encoded messages and have the same kind of problem that occurs when people see the body as a mere packaging for the soul. Art may be engaged and enjoyed deeply, even if one feels that its viewpoint is wrong. Philosopher Nicholas Wolterstorff in *Art in Action* (Grand Rapids: Eerdmans, 1980) has argued that artworks are material creations with rich aesthetic dimensions. He is critical of what he sees as the Protestant tendency to judge all art for its supposed religious views, even as he speaks of the necessity of discerning "the world behind the work"; see pp. 84-90.

25. Philip Pearlstein, "A Realist Artist in an Abstract World," in *Philip Pearlstein: A Retrospective* (Alpine, NY: Milwaukee Art Museum, 1983), p. 13.

Figure 4. Philip Pearlstein, *Two Female Models in Bamboo Chairs with Mirror* **(1981)**

connecting his work to a long tradition — predating nineteenth-century realism — of figurative studies that exist for their own sake and do not depend on extra visual sources, such as mythology. A significant difference between the earlier tradition and Pearlstein's work is his commitment to limitations. For instance, the drawings or prints of models by Rembrandt were only one part of a body of work that included portraits, biblical narratives, mythology, and historical subjects. By contrast, except for occasional portraiture, Pearlstein's subjects are almost entirely made up of the model in the studio. Because of his resolute refusal to have a hierarchy of meaning based on something other than sight, the models are not inherently more significant than other things in his visual field, and this gives the work a visual quality related to hard-edged abstraction done during the same period.

Pearlstein cares about his models as people, and he is not an advocate of a mechanistic view of the universe. But his artistic concerns are narrowly proscribed, so that bigger questions are literally not in the picture. At the end of the 1977 essay "A Realist Artist in an Abstract World," he asks,

> Does the fact that I see nature in abstract terms mean that the aesthetics of abstraction win in the struggle for my aesthetic soul? I suppose so, but in the course of my development I have learned to look at what is in front of me without idealizing it. That has been a consuming experience in itself, and ultimately that may be the aspect of my work that will continue to irritate. Most of us really don't want to see things as they are. Symbolist ideograms are easier to live with, but I am the IRS man of a few bodies that inhabit New York City and visit my studio periodically.[26]

One can almost hear the dry scratching of his visual audits.

One way to try to "see things as they are" is to disconnect the act of seeing from intrusive and bothersome extra-visual sources, as Pearlstein did by

26. Pearlstein, "A Realist Artist in an Abstract World," p. 15.

eliminating literary ideas, and for that matter almost everything that would situate the models in wider human experience. It seems obvious that this is not sight as it is used and experienced on a day-to-day basis. It is an essentialization of artistic scrutiny, and it separates the act of seeing from the act of understanding or interpreting the who and the what of the artist's subjects.

If Pearlstein is relentlessly single-minded in his attitude, photographer **Cindy Sherman** has explored her own image with similar intensity, but with markedly different effects. Her early work (fig. 5) was based on the black-and-white Hollywood studio stills of the 1940s and 1950s. In the 1980s, she turned to more elaborate large-format color prints, where the staging became theatrical and sometimes lurid, including a series using anatomical dummies and prosthetic body parts in grotesque and sexually violent situations. Sherman's work has been a critical and theoretical goldmine, because it touches so many sensitive and contentious areas within our culture. A *selected* bibliography in a 1997 monograph runs a full ten pages.[27] The ways in which Sherman's work has been analyzed revolve around the image and identity of women. Sherman's subjects — or rather our identification of the subjects in work that is all "untitled" — include celebrities, sex objects, victims (fig. 6), temptresses, housewives, hysterics, naifs, nurses, and other assorted traditional stereotypes of women. She is extremely adept at coordinating the ensemble of props, costumes, make-up, wigs, lighting, color, camera angle, lens distortion, pose, and facial countenance that seem to embody the stereotypic. But who and where is Sherman in all of this?

Figure 5. Cindy Sherman, *Untitled Film Still #7* **(1978)**

Michael Kimmelman, the senior art critic for the *New York Times,* noted that when he met Sherman he found that "it's almost uncanny how little she resembles any of her own pictures, even the ones that seem fairly straight forward."[28] While what interests

27. *Cindy Sherman: Retrospective* (New York: Thames and Hudson, 1997), pp. 208-17.
28. Michael Kimmelman, *Portraits: Talking with Artists at the Met, the Modern, the Louvre, and Elsewhere* (New York: Random House, 1998), p. 144.

Figure 6. Cindy Sherman, *Untitled #137* **(1984)**

a great deal of the critical community is the idea that her work critiques and undermines — deconstructs if you will — these very roles, Sherman herself is not so theoretically oriented. It is not that she is unfamiliar with the critical commentary, but rather that her attitude seems more direct and playful. In an interview where she was asked, "How do you get past all of the crap critics often write about you?" she responded, "Sometimes I've read stuff that never occurred to me." Later in the interview Sherman said, "I would read theoretical stuff about my work and think 'What? Where did they get that?' The work was so intuitive for me, I didn't know where it was coming from."[29]

Sherman is an artist who has some presence beyond the gallery and museum world. She has done work for *Vogue,* and one can buy posters of her pictures, the way one might of Van Gogh or Ansel Adams. I think a good part of the appeal of Sherman's art may be found in the way it resonates with the American cult of the self, and particularly the idea that we may *fashion* the self. Our media is clogged with images promising self-transformation, from cosmetics through dietary regimens to the plastic surgeon's "art." There is also the parallel spiritual and therapeutic marketplace, promising social confidence, inner peace, or relief from the sense that something's wrong or missing. Sherman's pictures, related as they are to commercial imagery, play off of the idea that we have the ability to pick and choose our self-image, and with that to create an identity. While her pictures may critique stereotypes, they seem to accept the malleability of personal identity as a given. In this aspect I believe they are an impressive example of our culture's confusion between one's image and one's identity.

For the academic and theoretical community, identity has been somewhat of an obsession, and Sherman's pictures seem to confirm that our identities are socially constructed. That is, our understanding of selfhood is dependent on the roles, beliefs, and power structures of the society we live in. The

29. Betsy Berns, "Studio: Cindy Sherman," *Tate Magazine,* Issue 5, http://www.tate.org.uk/magazine/issue5/sherman.htm.

old Western notion of human identity posited both a limited self and a core of character that was unique. That character certainly had flexibility and complexity, and might change dramatically in response to environmental pressures, but was understood to have some given, inherent qualities, either as an individual made in the image of God, or as a uniquely constituted physical and psychological persona. In both the Classical and Christian traditions, there was also profound recognition of human failing, which limited self-realization and provided the arts with some of their most compelling narratives.

Academic theory is characteristically complex, rife with references to other theorists, and apparently written to diminish any pleasure associated with reading. But it's important to recognize that pictures like Sherman's become illustrations for theories about human meaning and human relationships. Because Sherman's pictures raise questions about her own image, as well as the role of women, her work has been particularly attractive to critical theorists.[30]

The career of **Leon Golub** (1922-2004), the Chicago "monster roster" artist who was in the *New Images* exhibition, was neither as steady as Pearlstein's nor as mediagenic and celebrated as Sherman's. He was born around the same time as Pearlstein, and while he was active for many years, he achieved sustained recognition only in the late 1970s. In the 1950s he found living in New York difficult and the critical responses to *New Images* so painful that he and his wife, painter Nancy Spero, moved to Paris to find a more hospitable environment.[31] When he came back to the United States he was active in protests against the Vietnam War, and in the mid-1970s he suffered a crisis of confidence

about his work and came close to quitting as an artist. The work that people most readily associate with Golub are large paintings of mercenaries, riot police, torturers, or enforcers, which he began in the late 1970s (fig. 7). They are drawn from newspaper and television coverage of the civil wars, regional conflicts, and ethnic violence — El Salvador, Guatemala, South Africa, Rhodesia — that have been the constant background static against which Americans hear and see their own news.

If Sherman's work is easily interpreted in terms of its implicit political content, that content is still one of several possible points of entry. With Golub it is simply not possible to look at his paintings without confronting the politics of raw power, the place where rhetoric and ideology become force. The violence against overpowered bodies by self-satisfied hirelings who seem to enjoy their line of work is uncomfortably close. Our discomfort is abetted by both the large scale of the figures in a shallow, indeterminate space and the gestures and gazes of the perpetrators, who apparently want our approval, a bit like the way a cat may seek recognition as it offers an eviscerated bird.

Much of the overtly political art of the last thirty years has the one-dimensionality and evangelical fervor of fundamentalist tracts. Golub's work is far from detached, but there is an open-ended quality to it, as well as a concern for the craft of his trade that is unusual among politically oriented artists. Contemporary artists who seek to use art as a means of social address, with the attendant hope that attitudes and behaviors will change, often turn to the tools and imagery of mass media. Barbara Kruger, for instance, who had worked at Condé Nast

---

30. For example, in "Performing the Self as Other," an essay by Amelia Jones in *Interfaces: Women/Autobiography/Image/Performance* (Ann Arbor: University of Michigan Press, 2002), Jones argues first that we can't really know the artist from the work, which seems fairly logical. But she then goes on to argue: "Performing the particularly inflected (white, straight, Latina, Lesbian) female subject through the photographic pose, Sherman and Aguilar deploy the capacity of the photographic portrait to act as an *interface* — a site of exchange — and not only comment on the contingency of femininity (white, brown, or otherwise) on the gaze, but perform white heterosexual masculinity as lack" (p. 94).

It seems that Jones believes that Sherman's work not only critiques stereotypes of women, but also makes us aware of the "other" (ethnic or sexual minorities excluded from mainstream imagery) and demonstrates white male heterosexuality to be lacking. It seems fair to say that this kind of reading of Sherman — popular with critical theorists — depends as much on eisegesis, or a reading *into* the picture, as it does on exegesis, which tries to determine what is evident within the picture. Indeed, it seems to require a kind of *belief* before one can see what Jones attributes to Sherman's work.

31. Kimmelman, *Portraits*, p. 178.

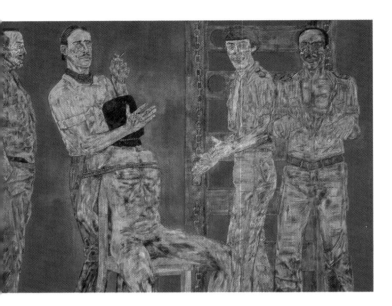

Figure 7. Leon Golub, *Interrogations II* (1980-81)

Figure 8. Barbara Kruger, *Untitled (Your gaze hits the side of my face)* (1981)

as a magazine designer, used her experience there to make commercially generated images that critique capitalism, the male gaze, and Classical aesthetics. (See fig. 8.)

Golub's paintings are rooted in the touch of the hand, as his surfaces are first painted and then abraded with solvents and implements that physically manifest pressure, wear, and force. They are also rooted in the long tradition of European history painting. But with Golub the celebration of nationalism (with its attendant triumphs and heroism) is inverted and the sordid reality on which political power so often rests is exposed, bereft of any rationale except "your body is the instrument on which my will may be done."

Western art, particularly Western Christian art, has a long history of depicting the body in extreme pain. But as the late painter Gregory Gillespie once noted, it is so familiar that we don't really see it: "You say 'oh that's Christ, or that's St. Paul — I know that story.' But if you look at Renaissance Art, Christian art, what percentage of the painting do you think involves somebody being assaulted? You know, a whole lot of Christian art."[32] In a similar fashion, as many media critics have argued, we are so accustomed to images of war, disaster, and mayhem, that we are anesthetized. It is Golub's considerable accomplishment that his painting can puncture the calloused skin of our apparent helplessness.

It seems that Golub's paintings might raise questions about the nature of suffering, affliction, and evil. In what context are we meant to see such pain? It is easy now to see that the "old" history paintings often justified evil in the name of the nation. But are all historical conflicts simply contests in the exercise of raw power? The art critic Donald Kuspit has noted, "Golub's history painting is not theodicy; it does not try to justify the evils of history in terms of some higher good. It is ugly."[33] It is ugly indeed, but must all suffering be shut off from "a higher good"? Is

32. Howard Fox and Arthur Lerner, "An Interview with Gregory Gillespie," in *Gregory Gillespie* (Washington, DC: Smithsonian Institution Press, 1977), p. 23.
33. Donald Kuspit, *Leon Golub: Existentialist/Activist Painter* (New Brunswick, NJ: Rutgers University Press, 1985), p. 81.

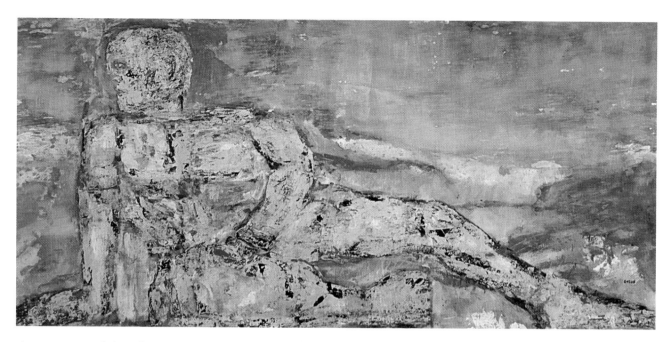

Figure 9. Leon Golub, *Reclining Youth* (1959)

there any possibility that one might fight for something good, or that suffering acts of evil may not always be tragic but might in fact be redemptive?

In light of the themes of *A Broken Beauty,* which posits that the Classical and Christian heritage have something to say to contemporary culture, it is significant that Kuspit's monograph on Golub deals extensively with the use of the Classical figure by the artist. In fact, the paintings by Golub that were exhibited in *New Images* drew directly from the Classical tradition. *Reclining Youth* (fig. 9), which was in the exhibit, is a reprise of *The Dying Gaul,* a third-century BCE Greek bronze, of which only a Roman copy still exists. For Kuspit, Golub's artistic stature is due to the "dialectic" between the Classical figure with its resonances of purpose, dignity, and transcendence, and "the devastating effect of modern man's sense of his ultimate meaninglessness, his absolute insufficiency, on his fundamental physical experience of being human."[34]

At this point it is useful to distinguish between the *figure* and the *body.* "Figure" denotes a received

34. Kuspit, *Leon Golub,* p. 14. The entire first essay in Kuspit's monograph, "The Classical/Contemporary Dialectic of Identity," wrestles with the language of the Classical past and how it may be legitimately used in a desacralized world.

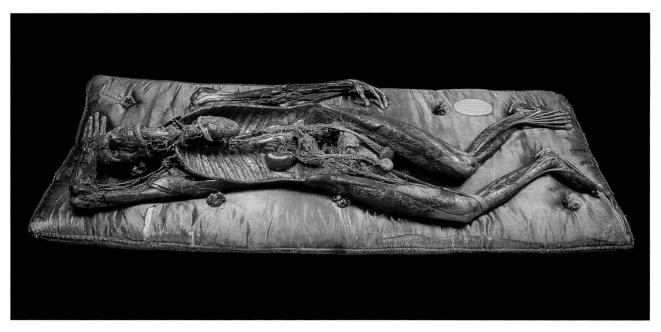

Figure 10. "System Lymphatica," from the *Encyclopedia Anatomica*

tradition of Western painting and sculpture. To speak of a "body" it is not necessary to invoke the tradition of the figure. Thus it is significant that in the last few decades the art world has taken to speaking about the body as an alternative to the figure. Critic Eric Gibson, writing about sculpture in the 1990s, succinctly delineated the difference, noting that "with the shift in focus to a mere physiological organism — the body — its evaporation into pure idea, and its enlistment in the social and political battles from which art was until recently kept apart, the figure in sculpture has severed its links with the humanistic tradition for whose values the human form has throughout the history of art served as a vehicle and spokesperson."[35] The Venice Biennale, which is the most prestigious international art exhibition, celebrated its one hundredth anniversary in 1995 with an extravagant exhibition devoted to exploring a century's worth of human images in terms of this idea.[36]

One of the artists that Gibson singled out for attention was **Kiki Smith**, daughter of the well-

35. Eric Gibson, "The Figure Reconsidered," *Sculpture,* May-June 1994, p. 10.
36. Jean Clair, Curator, *Identity-and-Alterity: Figures of the Body 1895/1995* (Venice: Marsillo, 1995). The official exhibition had 290 artists and a catalog of close to 600 pages.

known abstract sculptor Tony Smith. She grew up thinking of art in abstract terms, spending her childhood with her sisters "making little model octahedrons and tetrahedrons day after day after school."[37] She didn't see representational art until she went to college and took art history. Smith's family influenced her not only because through them she was exposed to artists and art but also because they had a Catholic heritage, so she knew the beliefs and practices of the church.

In 1980, Smith began to work with body imagery in a direct way. Smith has stated, "I think I chose the body as a subject, not consciously, but because it is the one form we all share; it's something we all have our own authentic experience with."[38] There is a kind of egalitarianism in this, because evidently only some people have the capacity to relate to the figurative tradition, but *everyone is* a body. That egalitarianism informs the way she looks at the body, which ignores social conventions regarding what is public or private and what is attractive or repellant. Smith's choice of low-tech materials like paper and wax and her generic reproductions of organs and systems gives her work a homemade yet clinical air. In 1985 she took a three-month EMS technician's course to acquaint herself better with the body's processes and internal systems.

There is not much in Smith's early work that directly relates to the Western tradition of the human form, except for artist's drawings made from dissections and collections like the anatomical studies in the Museo La Specola at the University of Firenze in Italy.[39] That extraordinary ensemble of eighteenth-century colored wax representations of organs, limbs, circulatory systems, skeletal structures, and splayed bodies (fig. 10) combine art, in the sense of the most demanding technical artistry,

Figure 11. Kiki Smith, *Untitled (A Man)* **(1988)**

37. Kimmelman, *Portraits*, p. 78.

38. Helaine Posner, *Kiki Smith* (New York: Bulfinch Press, Little, Brown and Co., 1998), p. 13. Biographical information about Smith is drawn from Posner's essay and interviews with Smith by David Frankel, all in *Kiki Smith*.

39. See *Encyclopedia Anatomica: Museo La Specola Florence* (Cologne: Benedict Taschen Verlag, 1999), which reproduces the collection and describes its formation and use.

with scientific study. By comparison, Smith's work appears provisional and crude, and that helps her images feel haunted by pathos. With her paper flayed skins (fig. 11) it is as though the formal and spiritual traditions of Western art had been evacuated, leaving only a deflated empty husk.

Smith has described the original intent of her skins in terms of abstraction. In a 1991 interview she said,

> What I wanted to do was to make just the form of it, without any content. They are just empty shells, and paper allowed me to make them very light, like they'd be if they were made of skin. . . . There's something Aquinas said about form being separated from matter, which is an underlying concern in my art. A lot of my work is about separating form from matter and kind of seeing what you've got. In a way, it was also the first time that I'd made a figurative sculpture because until then I'd always made sculptures of the internal organs. I'd never made the outside and I guess I was pretty frightened of the outside because I don't like personality. I just want to talk about the generic experience of the body without it becoming specific to specific people.[40]

In the same interview Smith said that the associations people made between her skins and spirituality, transcendence, and the loss of so many artists to AIDS came some time *after* her skins were made. This is a clear and interesting example of how an artist's work may come to represent something for a particular community, even though it was not made with that in mind.

Religion often hovers around discussions of Smith's work, since there is a material sensibility that is reminiscent of shrines or reliquaries, a display of some full figures that recall saints or Christ, and because Smith talks in interviews about the Catholic use of the body. Her later, full-body subjects draw on both myth and religion. In addition to *Lilith, Faeries,* and *Daphne,* she has made *The Virgin, Lot's Wife,* and a *Mary Magdalene.* The 1992 *Virgin Mary* (fig. 12)

resembles the écorché study figure used by art students, which has the skin and subcutaneous fat stripped off to better expose the musculature below. For Smith this is a way to emphasize the flesh, the pain, and the humanity of Mary, who, according to critic Eleanor Heartney, is robbed of her own flesh by becoming a vehicle for God's will.[41]

The *Virgin Mary* exemplifies the shift from figure to body. She has been stripped, both of her skin and of her symbolic attributes, and offers herself to us in mute discomfort. Whereas historically the figure of Mary was usually pictured as protecting, nurturing, comforting, or sorrowing over the body of her Son, these actions are not visible in the body before us. She seems, as Smith suggests in her interview, to be without personality. Mary's body becomes a sign to read in light of whatever knowledge one possesses about her. Given the traditional Catholic emphasis on Mary's purity, Smith's *Mary* appears de-immaculatized. Perhaps that's part of what Helaine Posner is getting at when she writes,

> One of Smith's most important contributions as an artist has been to reclaim the female body from patriarchy and to refigure it as the site of women's lived experience. This is not the fixed, self contained, or harmonious body of Classical art. It is the uncontrollable body that leaks, stains, defecates, and otherwise exposes its interior.[42]

Smith's attitudes toward Christianity and Catholicism are mixed. She has used the Virgin because she is one of her female superheroes, and because she wanted to do something positive. While she draws on Catholicism's sense of continuity between body and spirit, Smith is critical of what she sees as Christianity's overall contempt for physicality.[43] In one sense, she uses the body to *reconfigure* her Christian subjects in light of contemporary issues. Critic Eleanor Heartney counts her among artists like Robert

40. Carlo McCormick, "Kiki Smith," *Journal of Contemporary Art,* 1991, http://.jca-online.com/ksmith.html.

41. Eleanor Heartney, "Post-Modern Heretics," *Art in America* 85, no. 2 (February 1997): 37.
42. Posner, *Kiki Smith,* p. 20.
43. McCormick, "Kiki Smith."

Mapplethorpe, Andres Serrano (who made the infa-
mous *Piss Christ* photograph), and Joel Peter Witkin,
who were raised as Catholics. Heartney thinks their
Catholic past has oriented them to corporeality and
bodily imagery, even as they freely mix "the sacred
and the profane, which may appear as blasphemy
or sacrilege to fundamentalist viewers."[44] Speaking
of the culture wars, Heartney asks, "What would
happen if the battle were redefined not as a standoff
between believers and atheists, but between a Protestant, puritanically inclined fundamentalism, and
a more sensual and complex Roman Catholic–based
culture?"[45] This is the unhistorical simplification
described by art historian Sally Promey, and it seems
to overlook the fact that many Catholics — theoretically more sensual and complex — have been
offended too. But Smith's sculptures and Heartney's
interpretive desire live in the uneasy intersection
between art and religion that has received significant
publicity, but less comprehension, in the media and
the art world's critical community.

My point in choosing Pearlstein, Sherman, Golub,
and Smith is not to argue that they share common
ideas about the figure or the body. Generally they
don't. But there is scant talk about beauty in relation to their work, and they all appear to have more
discontinuity than continuity in relation to the art
of the Classical and Christian West. Any connection
between these artists and the past tends to gener-
ate discussions about how their work *differs* from its
antecedents, how it is *not* like that which it seemingly resembles. In one sense this is to be expected,
as all new art changes what came before. But the idea
of continuity within a tradition seems essentially
foreign to these artists, even if historical precedents
can be recognized in their work. It is worth consider-
ing *A Broken Beauty* in light of this, since, for all of
its contemporaneity, it seeks to engage and extend
the Christian tradition in Western art and looks to
the examples of artistic ancestors without the thick
myopic lens of critical theory.

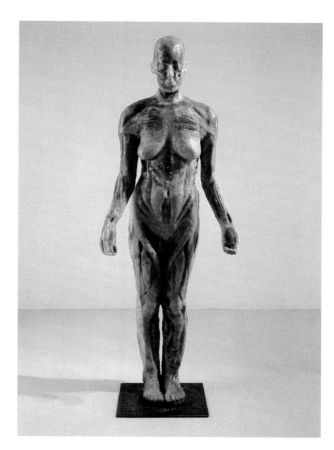

Figure 12. Kiki Smith, *Virgin Mary* **(1992)**

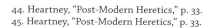

44. Heartney, "Post-Modern Heretics," p. 33.
45. Heartney, "Post-Modern Heretics," p. 33.

A Classical Revival?

While I believe that these four artists represent major attitudes toward the depiction and discussion of human imagery in our arts culture, I would be remiss not to point out that there are many figurative artists who do not subscribe to those attitudes. Some simply delight in the beauty, challenge, and complexity that the human subject affords. Others are united by a recent, renewed interest in Classicism. There are newly formed academies devoted to the recovery of Classical methods and traditions, galleries that solely exhibit Classical realism, and books that explore or promote the relationship between the art of the premodern West and our present moment. Charles Jencks's *Post-Modernism: The New Classicism in Art and Architecture* is likely the most thorough description of this resurgent Classicism, which he thinks began in the late 1970s.[46] Jencks casts a wide net and features artists like Edward Schmidt (fig. 13) who are visibly engaged with Classical forms and subjects. But there are also "ironizing" Classicists, "realist" Classicists (including Philip Pearlstein, who is prominently discussed), and "eclectic" Classicists. Since Jencks believes that there is both a "canonical" Classicism and a "free-style" Classicism that is difficult to define because of its polymorphous nature, it is hard to argue with his diverse inclusions.[47] Categorical borders *are* provisional and porous, but Jencks's work seems finally like a travelogue through the art of the period 1970 to 1987. His criteria for inclusion, as the title suggests, favors the eclecticism of postmodernity, with its ravenous appetite for looks and style. It is interesting to note that Christian subjects are noticeably absent from the book, since one might expect some Christian imagery to appear in the work of artists who have turned to the Western tradition for inspiration and source material.[48]

Jencks does invoke the idea of Christian rebirth to describe the impact Classical forms or ideas may have on the artist or architect who has rediscovered them.[49] He also speaks appreciatively of T. S. Eliot's idea of "the western tradition as an organic continuum — a reversible, living entity whose *past* could be changed by the introduction of a new link in the chain."[50] Both Eliot's idea and the first of Jencks's "New Rules" for Postmodern Classicism, which he describes as a new hybrid of "*dissonant beauty* or disharmonious harmony," have some relationship to *A Broken Beauty*.[51] But ultimately Jencks's view of the new Classicism seems too eclectic and too open to ambiguity, irony, or pastiche — oriented more to questions of form and style than to the recovery of the humanist vision.

The Classicism Jencks describes has much to admire. It has vivified the formal, technical, and historical vocabulary of artists. But I do not see a metaphysical or moral gravity in it that illuminates our human predicament. Perhaps it is unfair to judge all Classicists through Jencks's work. Yet overall the Classicism I have seen appears inflected with nostalgia, and even artists who purportedly address our human situation mythically, like Odd Nerdrum, appear largely given to fantasy and stylistic bombast. To me the figures of many Classicist works appear like time travelers from some imaginative past. So if one looks to the art of our times for insight into what it means to be human, what are the choices? Are we limited to dry description, critical rhetoric, unrelenting pain, and the endless, fragmenting mutability of social construction on the one hand, or an implicit longing for an archaic, pre-lapsarian past on the other?

The goal of *A Broken Beauty* is to be open to the present, with all of its messiness and confusion, but also to draw on the wisdom and examples of the Christian tradition. Thus beauty is not located in an alternate world, but something to be discerned within the disasters and dilemmas of our present cir-

---

46. Charles Jencks, *Post-Modernism: The New Classicism in Art and Architecture* (New York: Rizzoli, 1987), p. 12.
47. Jencks, *Post-Modernism*, p. 37.
48. Jencks, *Post-Modernism*. Possible Christian sources or interpretations are discerned occasionally, as in the discussion of Stephen Cox and Mimmo Paladino's work (pp. 57-58) or Stone Roberts's paintings (pp. 107-8).

49. Jencks, *Post-Modernism*, p. 318.
50. Jencks, *Post-Modernism*, p. 319.
51. Jencks, *Post-Modernism*, p. 330.

Figure 13. Edward Schmidt, *Oreads* (2000)

cumstances. Moreover, this is a loose enterprise. It is not organized by manifesto, confession, or creed, nor is it attempting to stake out stylistic or ideological turf like a movement. Rather, it is pulled together by a desire to see the *old* Christian image of humanity, with its core concepts of both sin and joy, inform the artistic figuration of our time.

Christian Reflection on the Body

This desire is not without problems. For one thing, there has not been much of a critical or interpretive community interested in engaging art on those terms. To the degree that the Christian tradition of the figure has been discussed, it has been largely limited to critiques of its inadequacy regarding gender equity and the representation of ethnicity. The organizer of *A Broken Beauty,* Bruce Herman, acknowledged this when he described his own preference for the word "body" in a paper given in 2003.

> Why "body" and not "figure"? One response to this question might read something like the following: in the art world the Figure is a term associated primarily with a masculine aesthetic tradition that has come down to us from the Europeans. It's inextricably interwoven with political might, subjugation of women, and the objectification of the body for erotic or other use. A more extreme answer might read: the figurative tradition is one of domination and control, and in order to rescue the human form from the totalizing and exclusively masculine aesthetic, it must now be referred to as the body — better yet, my body/your body instead of "the" body, because "the" body, again, has totalizing overtones. To a large extent, I am sympathetic to both these viewpoints, however extreme they might sound.[52]

If we admit that the figure is problematic, does the concept of a body help us? Is there a Christian view of the body?[53] Any discussion of the body in Christianity is bracketed by several related concepts. The first, found in the spare narratives of Genesis, declares that we are made in the image and likeness of God. But the narrative never tells *what* the likeness involves or how our image derives from God's. Various human capacities have been proposed by theologians and philosophers over the centuries, including our ability to communicate, our imaginative and creative potential, our ability to reason, our moral comprehension that distinguishes good from evil, our desire to enter into loving "I — thou" relationships, and our responsibility as a creature before a Creator.[54] Of course, this doesn't explain why we have bodies, or if our bodies are part of the image-bearing nature of our character, or why our bodies are subject to decay and death even as we long to live.

In biblical narratives the corruption of the body is the tangible fruit of sin, that most difficult of doctrines for contemporary culture. Though sin is the easiest Christian doctrine to verify — everybody knows something is disastrously wrong, and that the problem involves our choices and actions — the notion of guilt that has cosmic import abrades the sensibility of our desacralized, feel-good age. (Surely it is somebody else who is wrong.) Discussions of sin often lead to a consideration of God's character, with questions of why sin exists and whether that reflects a deficiency on the part of God's power or God's goodness. In my judgment the best engagement of these serious questions is found, not in the dialectics of debate, but in the *bodily* Incarnation of Christ, whom Christians believe to be fully human and fully divine.

The implications of the Incarnation for our own

---

52. Bruce Herman, "The Body, Beauty, and Brokenness," http://www.brucehermanonline.com/texts.html.

53. There are a growing number of books devoted to body theology, or the body as religiously conceived. *Religious Imagination and the Body* by Paula Cooey (New York: Oxford University Press, 1994) offers a feminist analysis. *The Theology of the Body* by Pope John Paul II (Boston: Pauline Books and Media, 1997) collects the Pope's writings and teachings on "Human Love in the Divine Plan."

54. Several of these ideas are summarized in Anthony Hoekema's *Created in God's Image* (Grand Rapids: Eerdmans, 1986). Dorothy Sayers, *The Mind of the Maker* (San Francisco: Harper, 1979), develops the idea that we are makers because God is a Creator.

embodiment are staggering. The author of the Gospel of John ends his book saying, "Jesus did many other things. If they were all written in books, I don't suppose there would be room enough in the whole world for all the books."[55] It is, as contemporary parlance puts it, impossible to get your mind around. For our purposes it is important to understand that in the Incarnation the universal experience of embodiment is affirmed in a most radical way. For those inclined to separate spirit from flesh, or to think that our ungainly bodies must be cosmeticized and corseted into an approximation of beauty, the Incarnation must be disturbing. It is too easy to abstract the "body of Christ" into a doctrine without confronting it as an individual life lived in the flesh, described without embellishment in the Gospel narratives.

The Gospels are narrated dramatically, and they all portray Christ's work as leading to his death. In fact, they seem to say that Christ's life is somehow *fulfilled* by that most degrading and disturbing of deaths. As the controversy over Mel Gibson's 2004 film *The Passion of the Christ* made clear, the purpose and point of Christ's death still provokes debate some two millennia after the event. Within the multiplicity of things that can be said about that death, two are critical for Christian reflection on embodiment.

One is that Christ's partaking of, or sharing in, the experience of embodiment up to and including a most gruesome death means that God is no stranger to pain. If Christ is indeed the visible embodiment of the person and character of God, we must puzzle over what his suffering means to us in light of that. There is a long history of Christian devotion and social action motivated by the desire to imitate the divine sharing in the brokenness of human life. Christians believe that God is not repelled by the ugliness of human life, and that belief necessarily reconfigures our own understanding of beauty and ugliness in terms of who people are and how we see them.

55. John 21:25, from the Contemporary English Version (New York: American Bible Society, 1995).

The other critical aspect of Christ's death that impinges on an understanding of embodiment is — if one believes the Gospel narratives — that death is not the end of our physicality. The resurrection of the body points to an essential unity of human experience. Embodiment is not something we pass through on the way to a higher consciousness. This belief has directed and sustained Christians over twenty centuries, and it must be reckoned as part of the psychological substrate that informed representations of the human body in Western art. Simply stated, there is reason to hope, because our circumstances now are not final.

It is important to look carefully at the bodies before us in contemporary art and to listen to what is said about them by their advocates. Criticisms of the biases and exclusions of earlier Western Christian art must be acknowledged and not waved away by appeals to tradition. But neither the criticisms of received traditions nor the return to formal or thematic aspects of Classicism provide adequate materials with which to fashion a new human image. We live now in the receding tide of Enlightenment hopes, which did so much to form the body of art — and the bodies in art — during the twentieth century. Our time looks to diminished horizons, and the resulting discomfort and disquiet are part of what shapes the bodies we see depicted around us.

Conclusion

A Broken Beauty raises many questions. One is whether the work will be seen as important enough *as art* to command attention. As we have seen, and as other essayists will confirm, assessments of what counts as important or noteworthy in art are not easily separated from attitudes and beliefs that originate outside of art. Thus, the more critical question *A Broken Beauty* poses is whether diverse works that are presented as religiously oriented can be seen as anything other than ideological within the contemporary arts culture. The difficulties the art world has had with religious imagery gives me reason to pause.

So it is necessary to affirm that the bodies before us in *A Broken Beauty* are not made to be ideological chits in a cultural polemic.

C. S. Lewis, the great Christian apologist and scholar of Medieval and Renaissance literature, gave his magisterial sermon "The Weight of Glory" at the Church of St. Mary the Virgin, in Oxford, in June of 1941. That sermon, given during England's dark days of World War II, was about the reality of the promise of heaven. Toward the end of the sermon Lewis turned from a consideration of heaven to the Christian's present responsibilities.

> It may be possible for each to think too much of his own potential glory hereafter; it is hardly possible for him to think too often or too deeply about that of his neighbor. That load, or weight, or burden of my neighbor's glory should be laid daily on my back, a load so heavy that only humility can carry it, and the backs of the proud will be broken.[56]

In some instances, the bodies depicted in *A Broken Beauty* are literally those of neighbors — family and friends. In other instances the bodies are metaphorically conceived. But all of the bodies speak of a desire for a human image that can carry the weight of complex meanings, where beauty is not a mask and brokenness is not the only reality. They are an artistic affirmation of the real presence Lewis described when, toward the end of his sermon, he admonished, "Next to the Blessed Sacrament itself, your neighbor is the holiest object presented to your senses."[57]

In *Pictures and Tears,* James Elkins describes the long Christian tradition of weeping in front of devotional images and the inability of art historical discourse to come to terms with the meaning of such art. It is sometimes easier to see art through the safety of professional categories than to confront its human implications. The point of the art in *A Broken Beauty* is not to make people cry. But it does bear empathetic witness to the commingling of beauty and brokenness in human life. Surely the exhibition will have accomplished its purpose if it helps us see the bodies before us as neighbors, not strangers.

56. C. S. Lewis, *The Weight of Glory and Other Addresses* (Grand Rapids: Eerdmans, 1966), p. 14.
57. Lewis, *The Weight of Glory and Other Addresses*, p. 15.

BROKEN BEAUTY, SHATTERED HEART
Timothy Verdon

2

The purpose of this book is to deal with beauty and brokenness in recent North American figurative art. The second of these themes is hardly surprising, after a century of horrors and at the beginning of a millennium inaugurated with devastating blows to our capacity to hope. But the first is unexpected: the very term "beauty" has an archaic sound, so long has it been absent from the theory and practice of contemporary art.

Still more unexpected is the *combination* of these terms in a single concept, apparently new, actually ancient. From Homeric times to Gustave Courbet, in fact, Western art explored the human experience of life as "beautiful," reserving places of particular privilege to the dignity people achieve through suffering. In a sense, the fallen heroes on red-figure vases and the *Funeral at Ornans* told the same kind of story, albeit from different points of view.

Then something happened. From Courbet through the 1980s, Western art seems no longer to have considered human dignity a "given," and significant movements in twentieth-century art disregarded the human image. Where found, that image was often bereft of beauty, nobility, or pathos. For over a century, in fact, the Classical and Christian roots of Western figurative art have been consciously rejected, caustically inverted, or simply ignored, and images born of other assumptions — Edvard Munch's *The Scream,* for example, with its haunting psychic isolation (fig. 1) — have achieved virtually iconic status.

Thus to find artists once again drawn by *both* suffering and hope — by human brokenness and human beauty — is startling, and it suggests that something is again "happening." It is something new, not just a return and still less a revival, but a kind of renascence: an authentic rebirth of concern for human beings.

And — astonishingly — this new interest in *the human* includes *God;* figuration and narrative again betoken a humanism rooted in the Christian dogma of Incarnation, which gives dignity and importance to every manifestation of life, even pain. The new interaction of beauty and vulnerability, indeed, echoes the biblical conviction that "God will not despise a shattered, humiliated heart" (Psalm 51:17).

Body and Soul, Art and Faith

"Beauty" and "brokenness" as treated in this volume presuppose a common tenet of both Classical and Christian thought: that *body* is an expressive vehicle — a sign, practically a sacrament — of *soul*. Bodiliness indeed is important, for Christians believe that in Jesus Christ God's eternal Word became *flesh* and lived among us, and "we saw his glory, the glory that is his as the only Son of the Father, full of grace and truth" (John 1:14).

"We saw": the point of Christ's Incarnation included *visibility:* we were meant to *see*. St. John repeats the Old Testament truth that "No one has ever seen God," but adds that "it is the only Son, who is nearest the Father's heart, who has made him known" (John 1:18). The point of Christ's assuming a body was in fact to make the invisible Father *seen,* because in *seeing* we *know* in a way that is near to the heart.

Christ made the Father's love visible, in a way that still deeply moves human hearts, above all when he gave his life for sinners, accepting death on a cross. There in the clearest way, in his visible body, he was, as the Letter to the Colossians calls him, "the *image* of the unseen God" (Colossians 1:15). When, after he had risen, he showed the wounds in his body to his disciples and ate with them to prove he

Figure 1. Edvard Munch, *The Scream* (1893)

**Figure 2. *Jesus and the Multiplication of the Loaves and Fishes*
(sixth century)**

was not a ghost, they finally understood the meaning of his mysterious claim to be able to rebuild the Jerusalem Temple, if it were to be destroyed, in three days. The evangelist John footnoted that assertion, explaining that the Lord had been "speaking of the sanctuary of his body" (John 2:21).

Thus, from the very beginning of Christian culture, the range of powerful religious meanings that in Judaism had been associated with the Temple found unification and fulfillment in the image of the body, and right from the start the assembly of Christ's followers, the Church, explicitly conceived itself as a "body" of which he is the head (Ephesians 1:22-23; Colossians 1:18; cf. Ephesians 5:23-32).

In the early centuries, this bodily focus was often more theological than visual, however. In its developing stages, Christian art was uneasy with our corporeal condition, often preferring symbolic images, such as the Chi-Rho (the Greek initials of the word "Christ"), or the fish, similarly allusive to the name of Christ. Nor is it hard to grasp why such aniconic formulae became popular, as Christian art began to distinguish itself from Greco-Roman prototypes: images, and above all images depicting the body, were associated with paganism and must have retained idolatrous connotations for early Christians, not least because many believers had died for their faith when they refused to offer sacrifice before statues of the ancient gods or of the deified emperor.[1]

Early Christianity's rejection of the body was also grounded in its sense that the pagan world had "exchanged the glory of the immortal God for a worthless imitation, for the image of mortal man, of birds, of quadrupeds and reptiles," as St. Paul asserts (Romans 1:23), and had been abandoned by God "to degrading passions" (cf. Romans 1:26-27). Indeed, the first chapter of Paul's Letter to the Romans states unambiguously how early Christians viewed

---

1. This thumbnail outline of Christian art is an extreme synthesis of Timothy Verdon, "L'occhio spirituale. Il contributo del cristianesimo all'arte," in *Dopo 2000 anni di Cristianesimo*, edited by the Servizio Nazionale della Conferenza Episcopale Italiana per il Progetto Culturale (Milan: A. Mondatori, 2000), pp. 231-64; and Timothy Verdon, *L'arte sacra in Italia. L'immaginazione religiosa dal paleocristiano al postmoderno* (Milan: A. Mondatori, 2001).

the bodily immorality to which the statues of the old gods often alluded.

Two consequences are apparent in the visual arts. The first is a practically total refusal, within the early Church, of monumental sculpture, the most "bodily" of artistic media and that most obviously associated with idolatry. In barely a century, between the early fourth and the fifth centuries, what had been the main art form of the Mediterranean world for a thousand years, the powerful plastic projection of the masculine or feminine body in imposing works of marble and bronze statuary, simply disappeared.

The second consequence was more subtle. When the body *was* represented, it was spiritualized. Instead of free-standing monumental statues, we now find low relief on a small scale or mosaic; instead of classical nudity or semi-nudity, fully draped figures; and in place of the moody introspection of Hellenistic and Roman statues, alert but somewhat impersonal gazes into eternity in fifth- and sixth-century figures at Ravenna and elsewhere.

This loss of physical solidity in Christian art of the late Patristic era is related to a "dissolution" of narrative concreteness in the treatment of subject. Where Classical art had used realistic bodies to tell stories in intelligible ways, Christian art of this period and for much of the Middle Ages preferred treating the body as symbol within the framework of a mystagogy little concerned with narration. Thus, for example, *Jesus and the Multiplication of the Loaves and Fishes* in Sant'Apollinare Nuovo, Ravenna (fig. 2), presents the New Testament miracle in initially puzzling terms — an imperially robed figure in cruciform pose distributing bread and fish to his apostles — which oblige us to seek meanings beyond the event itself. Christ's posture here in fact connects this manifestation of his power to nourish with the ultimate gift of his body and blood as real food and drink in the *Pascha Domini* — the gift made in sacramental form at the Last Supper and in bodily form on Calvary — and the gold-bordered purple toga suggests his glory as risen *Kyrios, Dominus,* Lord. The literal account of loaves and fishes has less importance, here, than the theological presentation

of a Savior whose every earthly act pointed toward his death and resurrection. And the body in which earthly acts are accomplished now serves to illustrate that higher purpose, its natural expressiveness replaced by poses and movements alluding to ideas.

This sign language perfected by the early Church proved especially useful in the spread of Christianity to lands and peoples outside the cultural pale of Mediterranean Classicism. Franco-German and Celtic artists, who preferred stylized animal forms and geometric or zoomorphic decoration, could deal more effectively with symbols than with the human body. Even when Northern artists rediscovered the body as subject (from the Carolingian era through the Romanesque and Gothic ages), their sensibility remained colored by abstract formal considerations and overall elegance of design more than by interest in the body as it is in nature; the angular choreography of Romanesque relief figures from Vézelay in Burgundy to Santo Domingo in Silos, Spain, makes the point.

Invention of the Christian Body

It was in Italy, between the end of the twelfth and the middle of the thirteenth centuries, that a dramatic and — for the West — decisive process of change began. Art rediscovered the body in fully religious terms, as a privileged vehicle of spiritual experience, *locus* of a uniquely Christian sanctity. This amazing evolution, which stretches from Benedetto Antelami to Michelangelo and Titian, defined the modern European vision of humanity, once and for all distinguishing Occidental culture from that of the Christian East.

The change in art came in response to a change in Western spirituality traditionally associated with St. Francis of Assisi, whose deeply human style of Christian life put a premium on emotional and physical experience. An early work produced for Francis's followers, a painted cross in the Franciscan church in Arezzo, perhaps attributable to a local master, can suggest the saint's "style."

Figure 3. Detail of *Painted Cross with St. Francis* by anonymous Aretine master (ca. 1260)

While the monumental body of Christ is still Byzantine in inspiration and the figure of Francis at Christ's feet has an angular contortion not unlike the Romanesque relief sculptures just mentioned, the artist has gone to considerable lengths to coordinate Francis's bent pose with the action in which he is engaged as he reverently holds and kisses Christ's right foot, bathed in blood and with the nail clearly visible (fig. 3). This profound awareness of Christ's pain is a matter of mind (we note the saint's intelligent gaze) and of heart (we are struck by the tenderness with which he presses his lips to Christ's foot), but also of *body,* for Francis so fully identifies with his Lord that Christ's very wounds have appeared in his hands and feet: the panel shows the same kind of black mark in Francis's left hand as in Christ's right foot.

The lower part of the image offers a still more remarkable detail. The crimson blood flowing from Christ's left foot, given particular evidence by the black background, reaches Francis's own foot as it rests on the hard rock of Golgotha. Christ's blood arrives at Francis's foot and then continues below it, but does not flow *over* St. Francis's foot! Rather — we are meant to understand — the blood of Christ flows *through* Francis's foot: through the wound of the stigmata; through the passage that compassionate love had opened in Francis's flesh! It is a kind of transfusion, the blood of God in a man, Francis, who with St. Paul can affirm: "I live now not with my own life but with the life of Christ who lives in me" (Galatians 2:20).

This astounding visual assertion that Francis was indeed — as his followers maintained — an *alter Christus,* "another Christ," has ample parallels in the early Franciscan literature. St. Bonaventure, speaking of the stigmata in his *Life of Francis* commissioned by the Order, says that Francis had spent forty days and forty nights on Mount La Verna (the allusion to Moses on Horeb would have been apparent to his readers), descending finally with God's law, not on tablets of stone or wood but graven into his own flesh by the finger of the living God.

The new law — Christ's law of a love so great it can accept death for others — is written in human flesh! It was novel and irrefutable proof of the worthiness of the flesh, of its eternal value, of the dignity of human beings who are soul but also *body*. We are thus not surprised by the rediscovery, in approximately the same years as the Arezzo cross, of the body in art and indeed of the classically proportioned, heroic body: well known is the small *Hercules* or *Daniel* of Nicola Pisano's pulpit for the Baptistery in Pisa (fig. 4).

So acute was the hunger to see the body as part of a spiritual quest that the old prohibition on nature was lifted, and Greco-Roman art was pressed back into service. We should note, however, that this precocious Italian reuse of ancient prototypes was not only or primarily a matter of learned revival but above all of Christian renewal: the Bishop of Pisa who commissioned Nicola Pisano's pulpit, Federico Visconti, is known to have been an ardent admirer of St. Francis, whom he had met personally in his youth.[2]

Nicola Pisano himself developed these insights in the second of his pulpits, that made for Siena Cathedral in 1265, where the sensitive modeling of Christ's body and the pathos of his inner state are light years beyond what any painter, Cimabue and Duccio included, would do in the following decades (fig. 5). Only Giotto surpassed Nicola's achievement, which in a sense he incorporated, since Giotto's underlying values are as sculptural as they are pictorial (fig. 6).

The Development of Christian Humanism

From Nicola Pisano and Giotto in the late thirteenth and early fourteenth centuries, men and women, their world, their relationships, and their spiritual nature became not only the prevailing subjects of European art but practically the only ones.[3] Even

Figure 4. Detail of a baptistery pulpit in Pisa by Nicola Pisano (1260)

Figure 5. Detail of Christ on the cross from a pulpit by Nicola Pisano in Siena Cathedral (1265-67)

2. C. Piana, "I sermoni di Federico Visconti, Arcivescovo di Pisa," *Rivista di storia della Chiesa in Italia* 6 (1952): 231-48; E. M. Angiola, "Nicola Pisano, Federico Visconti, and the Classical Style in Pisa," *The Art Bulletin* 59 (1977): 1-27.

3. Verdon, *L'arte sacra in Italia*, pp. 76-83; Verdon, "Christianity, the Renaissance and the Study of History: Environments of Experience and Imagination," in *Christianity and the Renaissance: Image and Religious Imagination in the Quattrocento,* ed. Timothy Verdon and John Henderson (Syracuse, NY: Syracuse University Press, 1990), pp. 1-40.

Figure 6. Giotto, *Crucifixion* (ca. 1305)

Figure 7. Filippo Lippi, *Madonna and Child* (ca. 1430)

when other subjects — landscape and still life — later came to be accepted, their rendering still implied the human subject, since it obeyed optical laws and elicited feelings that are part of a *human* perception of the world. From Giotto to the Impressionists, we might say, works of figurative art functioned as "windows" through which men and women contemplated a universe peculiarly their own: the natural world, the body, the soul.

We should remember that, in its beginning, this art was *religious*, fashioned for the liturgy and for personal devotion. The images it offered were thus "sacred," drawing meaning from the system of faith within which the images functioned. The countless representations of the Madonna with child, for instance (fig. 7) — or of historical subjects like the baptism of Christ (fig. 8) — gave the human figure a centrality and dignity explicitly related to the dogma of Incarnation.[4] The image of the child, playful or quiet in his mother's arms, and that of the classically beautiful man, affirmed Christian faith that in Jesus born of Mary the fullness of divinity coexists with the fullness of humanity. The beauty Renaissance artists gave Christ expresses this incomparable dignity of the human being, whose nature God assumed, and the realism of their details — contemporary dress and everyday objects — extends the dignity to earthly surroundings, implying a sanctity in all things.

When, moreover, as in the statuesque Christ in Piero della Francesca's *Baptism*, the beauty depicted derived from Ancient art, it implies a continuity both with the past (Classical Antiquity) and with other systems of belief (Olympian paganism). In Jesus' Apollo-like beauty, Piero seems to say, the Greco-Roman equation of physical comeliness with divinity is vindicated and the cult of the old gods revealed as preparation for the gospel.

Such Christian humanism had an ontological concreteness — an "objectivity" — related to its

4. Marilyn A. Lavin, *Piero della Francesca's* Baptism of Christ (New Haven and London: Yale University Press, 1981); Timothy Verdon, "Symbol and Subject in Piero's *Baptism of Christ*," in *Musagetes. Festschrift für Wolfram Prinz*, ed. Ronald Kecks (Berlin: Mann Verlag, 1991), pp. 245-53.

function. The *Baptism of Christ* (fig. 8), for example, was originally an altarpiece in the monastic church of San Giovanni Evangelista at the gates of Borgo San Sepolcro. This image of the body assumed by God was meant to be seen over an altar where bread and wine became the body and blood of God's Son. And the relation to the distant past, implicit in Piero's evocation of ancient statuary, asserted itself within a liturgical context where sequential time in fact is overcome when the "past" event of Calvary is made "present" in the Eucharist. In much the same way, the dazzling vision of nature that Piero constructed around Christ's body was meant to be seen in relation to elements drawn from nature: the bread and wine which become that body. In Piero's Christ, therefore, human beauty was put in relation with history, with remote cultures, and with the cosmos.[5]

Above all, in the Renaissance tradition humanity is pictured in relationship — with others, with oneself, and with God. Piero's Christ accepts baptism from St. John; he fully understands the implications of his action and accepts its consequences; he hears the words pronounced by his heavenly Father: "You are my beloved son. In you I am well pleased" (Luke 3:22). Piero's image — of a man standing firm against the backdrop of history and the world — is in fact an icon of liberty, of conscious commitment, and of relatedness in love. The gravely serious facial expression (fig. 9) tells us that Christ knows himself summoned to another "baptism," as he later calls the cross, where he will have to descend not into water but into death. He knows this, accepts it, and feels the closeness of the Father, which he later describes: "The spirit of the Lord is upon me, wherefore he has anointed me to preach the gospel to the poor, to preach deliverance to captives and sight to the blind, to set at liberty them that are bruised, to preach the acceptable year of the Lord" (Luke 4:18-19; cf. Isaiah 61:1-2).

Piero's noble Christ and similar early Renaissance images prepare the way for those supreme state-

5. On these themes, and more generally on the relationship of medieval and Renaissance art to the liturgy, see Timothy Verdon, *Vedere il mistero. Il genio artistico della liturgia cattolica* (Milan: A. Mondadori, 2003).

Figure 8. Piero della Francesca, *Baptism of Christ* (ca. 1450)

Figure 9. Detail of Francesca's *Baptism of Christ:* the face of Christ

Figure 10. Gianlorenzo Bernini, *Cardinal Scipione Borghese* (ca. 1632)

ments of beauty and pathos that we associate with High Renaissance and Baroque masters: Leonardo, Michelangelo, and Raphael; Dürer and Grünewald; Giorgione and Titian; Rubens, Rembrandt, and Bernini. In European art of these centuries, moreover, even when the subject is not formally religious (as in Rembrandt's or Bernini's portraits) we sense an enveloping humanity — a compassion and even humor — best explained in light of the Judeo-Christian worldview shared by artists and patrons alike. Bernini's sensitive, ebullient *Cardinal Scipione Borghese,* for example, known in two carved versions for which there is an extraordinary drawn study in the Pierpont Morgan Library (fig. 10) and a comical "alternative vision" of the plump prelate in the Vatican Library, irradiates warmth, understanding, and the genuine friendship that linked Bernini to the churchman.

In the same way, the anthropocentric presentation of nature, which in Piero's *Baptism* has obvious theological significance, showing Christ at the center of a world in which "not one thing had its being but through him" (John 1:3), leads directly to what is often called "classical landscape" painting, in which mountains and valleys, sky and sea express the harmony or turmoil imaginable in the hearts of human actors (fig. 11). From Giorgione's *Tempest* to Annibale Carracci, Nicholas Poussin, Claude Lorraine, and eighteenth- and early nineteenth-century masters, the outer world mirrors our inner state, as if in literal confirmation of St. Paul's claim that "the whole creation is eagerly waiting for God to reveal his sons [and] still retains the hope of being freed, like us, from its slavery to decadence" (Romans 8:19-21).

The obvious question — whether such features could have developed apart from Christianity — is unanswerable and ultimately idle, since in fact they did not. Greco-Roman art offers no real parallels, nor do the visual cultures of non-Western peoples, to the peculiar human beauty and pathos suggested above which are fruits of a civilization that for more than a thousand years meditated on the Bible and celebrated the Eucharist. That there were also other, nonreligious influences on these developments is beyond doubt, but so is the fact that the core of Western culture for centuries was Christian.

The Crisis of Humanism

At a given point in time, however, this long tradition died, and the image, which Western civilization had perpetuated in art since the Middle Ages, became obsolete. Not only religious subjects, like Piero's *Baptism of Christ,* but images of free human beings committed to the good and inspired by Someone or something above or outside their own interests, gave way to other, more "modern" images: of doubt; of fragmentation of the individual; of conditioning factors that diminish or even annihilate humankind.

A very early instance of the new mood is Caspar David Friedrich's *Wayfarer,* a work of 1818 (fig. 12). This image of a gentleman who stops to contemplate the vastness of a mountain landscape captures all the Romantic sense of nature as sublime but also as totally "other": distant from the human subject, overwhelming. While, from the Renaissance onward, landscape painting had been developed in relation to men and women, Friedrich here emphasizes the immensity of space and an anonymity (or at least inscrutability) in the human subject, who seems to say: "Before all this, what is man?"[6] The epochal political and social upheavals of the time, and the titanic figure of Bonaparte, had clearly disturbed some inner balance, shattered some fundamental trust, and when individuals now sought comfort in nature, they found themselves face to face with uncontrollable forces, too imposing in their absolute simplicity to be grasped by intelligence.

In Friedrich's painting the reaction of the anonymous subject is not *religious,* at least not in any traditional way. His attitude does not suggest prayer, and his modern clothes, peculiar to a gentleman of the early nineteenth century, situate this encounter in

6. Fritz Novotny, *Painting and Sculpture in Europe, 1780-1880,* The Pelican History of Art (Harmondsworth, Middlesex: Penguin Books, 1971), pp. 95-101.

Figure 11. Nicolas Poussin, *Landscape with Saint John on Patmos* (1640)

Figure 12. Caspar David Friedrich, *The Wayfarer* (1818)

Figure 13. Eugène Delacroix, *The Death of Sardanapalus* (1827)

Figure 14. Edgar Dégas, *The Absinthe Drinker* (1876)

a framework of philosophical or scientific reflection, perhaps related to the quasi-pantheistic nineteenth-century impulse toward "natural Christianity." A scientist of the following generation, John Tyndall (1820-1893), would describe a similar experience on the Matterhorn, where the grandeur of the mountain set him to pondering the millenary geological processes of formation and erosion of the stone and the meteorological causes of the fog that blankets that mountain. Tyndall asked himself whether his subjective reactions — sadness, and a sense of fatality — were somehow an extension to his consciousness of the same physical processes he saw in nature.[7]

The nineteenth and twentieth centuries in effect redefined our relation to the universe. Friedrich's musing gentleman, painted in 1818, is contemporary with Arthur Schopenhauer's essay *The World as Will and Representation;* Tyndall's meditation on the Matterhorn in 1868 unfolded five years after T. H. Huxley's *The Place of Man in Nature* (1863) and nine years after Darwin's *Origin of Species* (1859).

This nineteenth-century search for a new relation to nature — that is, to the physical universe — has an exact parallel in the period's exploration of *human nature:* of its moral and ethical limits, of the "possible" types of behavior for a human being. In art, for example, direct contact with Eastern cultures, fascination with the exotic, and a taste for strong sensations led Eugène Delacroix to turn a tragedy by Byron into the famous painting for the Salon of 1827, depicting a Persian satrap who — from his state bed — ordered the slaughter of his concubines and page boys, even of his favorite horse: *The Death of Sardanapalus* (fig. 13).[8] Anticipating the historicized violence of modern film, Delacroix offers a neo-Baroque analogue for the atrocities of the French Revolution (which he may have remembered: he was born in 1787). The attraction of evil, the tidal swell of unfettered passion, the idolatry of luxury, power, and cruelty stand out clearly in this painting.

It was, obviously, an age of dramatic, even violent

7. Quoted in J. W. Burrow, *The Crisis of Reason: European Thought, 1848-1914* (New Haven: Yale University Press, 2000), p. 42.
8. Novotny, *Painting and Sculpture in Europe,* pp. 151-65.

change. The 1830 July Revolution and consequent political and economic situation kindled implacable resentment in Europe's liberals, unleashing a Continent-wide series of uprisings in whose heat Marx and Engels published the *Communist Manifesto*.[9] Among participants in the "troubles" of 1848-49 were two whose writings shed light on modern art's rejection of the traditional concept of the order of the universe with humanity at its center. In Dresden, in 1848, we find both Richard Wagner and Mikhail Bakunin, the musician and the terrorist, both thirty-five years old and involved in an unsuccessful revolt against the Saxon government. Bakunin had already expressed in print his belief that "the passion for destruction is a creative passion";[10] and in 1849, in an unsigned article written by Wagner, "Revolution" would speak in the first person, proclaiming: "I am the dream, the balm, the hope of all who suffer. . . . I shall destroy any illusion which has power over men. I shall destroy the supremacy of the one over the many, of the dead over the living, of matter over spirit. . . . I am the only god whom all the universe recognizes."[11] Between 1849 and 1852, Wagner then wrote two essays that would greatly influence Nietzsche and consequently the entire late nineteenth and early twentieth century: *Art and Revolution* and *The Artwork of the Future*.

On one hand was destruction as a creative act; on the other, art that must cause revolution, mold the future, live up to messianic expectations in a world without God. (*The Artwork of the Future* was dedicated to Ludwig Feuerbach, who in 1844 had published *The Essence of Christianity,* claiming that every religion is illusion and religious ideas are mere images that people fabricate to deal with reality.)

Other uprisings subsequently improved the lot of workers, but — in a world without God — also triggered new social issues; in the huge, overcrowded, and anonymous cities of the end of the nineteenth century nervous depression, alienation, alcoholism, and other spiritual pathologies spread. Degas'

L'absinthe of 1876 and, later, the paintings, drawings, and prints of Toulouse Lautrec describe this atmosphere well (fig. 14).

Building Emptiness

The moral void created *around* and *in* men and women of the late nineteenth century was prepared by the political, social, and spiritual revolutions evoked above. The suffering caused by this void, and by the *petit bourgeois* respectability that was the only apparent fruit of the revolutions — the moral and social hypocrisy of a life based on lies that Heinrich Ibsen describes — is attested by Ibsen's fellow citizen, the Norwegian Edvard Munch. Munch lost his mother when he was fourteen and was brought up by his father, a doctor in the royal army, extremely devout and rigorous, against whom Edvard rebelled, becoming a painter and joining the Bohemia of Christiania youth movement, which repudiated the social and sexual conventions of its day. Munch's autobiographical painting *The Scream* of 1893, made shortly after the artist's return from a period in Paris, is the most famous of his works (see again fig. 1); it illustrates, in the language of French symbolism, a moment of unbearable anguish, later described verbally by the artist: "I stopped and leaned against the railing, dead tired. Above the blue-black fiord hung clouds as red as blood or tongues of flame. My friends had left me, and, alone, trembling with distress, I felt the vast, endless cry of nature."[12] If we recall another painting of a man moved at the sight of nature — Caspar David Friedrich's *Wayfarer* (see above, fig. 12) — we can compute the inner distance between the nineteenth century's beginning and its end. Between Friedrich's painting of 1818 and Munch's of 1893 stretch seventy-five years in which the search for a new place in the universe had finally produced horror. Physical science (which by Friedrich's day had already replaced religious faith)

9. Burrow, *The Crisis of Reason*, pp. 1-30.

10. E. H. Carr, *Michael Bakunin* (London, 1975), p. 110.

11. Ernest Newman, *The Life of Richard Wagner,* 4 vols. (London, 1933-46), vol. 2, pp. 55-56.

12. George Heard Hamilton, *Painting and Sculpture in Europe, 1880-1940,* The Pelican History of Art (Harmondsworth, Middlesex: Penguin Books, 1967), pp. 122-29.

had now given way to psychology, and the immensity of an alienated cosmos no longer excited admiration but only the echo — in the narrow spaces of the human spirit — of an equally "cosmic" alienation.

The social and spiritual illnesses of the nineteenth century derived in part from a systematic demolition of every myth structure on which the culture of previous ages had rested. The first to fall (because it was the most recent, dating back only to the Renaissance) was the "classical" structure; a famous drawing by Henry Fuseli evokes its decline poetically, showing an artist in tears before the ruins of the past.

The privileged position of Greco-Roman culture, which from the sixteenth through the eighteenth centuries had given Europeans a sense of historical rootedness in their own cultural life, was challenged by increasing familiarity with Eastern and "primitive" cultures from the beginning of the nineteenth century onward. And while, in the Renaissance, the theological framework of Christianity had allowed the assimilation of new data furnished by archaeological and philological discoveries, the nineteenth century's emerging scientific mentality led only to taxonomic classification; the second part of the century would in fact see a proliferation of departments of ethnography and of anthropology in European and American universities and museums.

The importance of the Greco-Roman past for the construction of the present, unquestioned from Dante to Diderot, was thus fatally relativized; and the values implied in individual and collective behavior, as well as the social ideals inherited from Athens and Rome, could no longer claim the authority they had once enjoyed.

The implications of this collapse for the other supportive structure of European identity, Christianity, were immense. On one hand, the new, "alternative" systems of faith and morals (unlike Greco-Roman civilization) had no organic links with the beginnings of Christian culture, which thus suffered its own process of relativization, no longer perceiving itself as the "natural" synthesis of Greek and Hebrew ideas in a composite reality that reflected the entire past, but as only one system among many. In addi-

tion, nineteenth-century anthropology accepted Darwin's idea of "cultural progress," which, together with the new science of sociology developed by Herbert Spencer and later Emile Durkheim, gave an objective basis to liberal hostility toward institutions of the *ancien régime,* above all the Church.

These attitudes, which at the level of mass culture still used the anticlerical language of the Enlightenment, are anticipated in the introduction to a work published in Paris in 1847, *Les mystères de l'Inquisition,* in which the author informs his public that "for twenty centuries the world had been handed over to tyrants, that is to kings and priests," of course showing scenes of the Spanish Inquisition.[13] Feuerbach had already used this approach with Protestantism, as did Spencer with Anglicanism in Great Britain. Auguste Comte, disciple of the socialist Henri de Saint-Simon (founder of the so-called *Nouveau Christianisme* of the 1820s), published his *System of Positive Philosophy* in 1854, presenting a new religion made of science, progress, and *humanité.* Ten years later Jules Michelet became its apostle with his bestselling *Bible de l'Humanité.*

"We must do an about-face," Michelet wrote,

> and rapidly and courageously turn our backs on the Middle Ages: on that morbid past which contaminates us with death. Do not fight it, do not criticise it, simply forget it! Forget it and move on to the sciences of life, to the museums, to the schools, to the Collège de France! Interrogate Antiquity, which we know well from recent expeditions: there shall we learn to be human. Night's shadows are dissolving, and on the solid basis of nature and history, Justice shines eternal.[14]

Material Myth and *Décadence*

For those who chose not to "forget" Christianity, there were problems of a different sort. If the popular *Life of Jesus* published in 1835 by the German

13. M. Féreal, *Les mystères de l'Inquisition* (Paris, 1847), p. 1.
14. Jules Michelet, *Bible de l'Humanité* (Paris, 1864), pp. 207, 483.

David Friedrich Strauss practically disregarded the historical figure, reducing Christ to a pure concept, a privileged moment in some Hegelian scheme of development of the universal mind, then the "biography" signed by Ernst Renan in 1863 imprisoned Christ in the historical circumstances of his age, reducing him to a mere man — fascinating, a master of humanity — but no more than human. Renan considered Christ outstanding, one of the "greats" of world spiritual history, but not unique, not the definitive presence of all times, capable of enlightening every aspect of human life.

Thus the New Testament, like the Old before it, was reduced to a historical novel whose plot artists might exploit. A famous example is Gustave Moreau's *Apparition of John the Baptist's Head to Salome* of 1876, which inspired Oscar Wilde's tragedy on the subject (forbidden by the British authorities but presented by Sarah Bernhardt in Paris in 1894). In Moreau's painting, as in Wilde's play, the Precursor of the Christian gospel gets lost amid luxuriant Orientalism and erotic intrigue (fig. 15).

In addition, nineteenth-century ethnographic studies stimulated interest in alternative myth systems, such as the German and Scandinavian legends retold in Wagner's *Niebelungenlied* and the Anglo-Celtic cycle of King Arthur. The brothers Grimm, James Frazer, and again Renan repopulated the European imagination with gods, heroes, and mysterious princesses with magic powers encountered in dark woods by misty lakes. The rediscovery of pre-Christian and early Medieval myths and legends was moreover part of a new nationalism promoted by the two main powers, Great Britain and — especially after its unification under Wilhelm I and Bismarck in 1870 — Germany, the pseudo-historical background offered by legend contributing to shape racial theories, which, particularly in Germany, became part of a sense of national vocation.

Within this framework, Christianity became simply one of the many systems in which people had expressed themselves in the "elementary" stages of their cultural evolution. In this spirit, Gaugin's *Vision After the Sermon* of 1888 shows how simple women

Figure 15. Gustave Moreau, *Apparition of St. John the Baptist's Head to Salome* (1876)

Figure 16. Paul Gaugin, *The Vision After the Sermon* (1888)

Figure 17. Emil Nolde, *Dance Around the Golden Calf* (1910)

from the Breton countryside "visualize" the fight between Jacob and the Angel of which their parish priest had spoken at Mass (fig. 16); done in the new "symbolist" style, the painting suggests how to interpret myths: the biblical event, reduced to a vignette in the upper right corner of the image, has little importance in itself, and we see it "from the perspective of" or "through" credulous village women with heads wrapped in archaic bonnets — the Word of God as folklore.

Three years later, Gauguin left for Tahiti in search of other myths. In several of his Tahitian works we find the invitation to women: *"Soyez amoureuses, vous serez heureuses"* ("Be amorous and you'll be happy"), words that express the ultimately dominant myth of the nineteenth and twentieth centuries, the belief that sex, freed from Judeo-Christian moral restraints, makes people happy and, indeed, more human, more able to relate to themselves, to others, and to nature.

The high priest of this religion was Friedrich Nietzsche. In 1872, in *The Birth of Tragedy,* Nietzsche located the source of art in the artist's self-abandonment to "dionysiac" sensuality. Rejecting both the rationalism of ancient Greece and the Christian ideal of selfless love, Nietzsche would further claim — in *The Twilight of the Idols* — that true art must express the liberation of the individual person, the prerequisite of which (thus also a prerequisite of personality) is *rapture.*

"Intoxicating rapture must bring about excitement in the whole human mechanism," Nietzsche wrote; "artistic creativity cannot exist without rapture. All types of rapture, even with different origins, have this power, but particularly the rapture of sexual arousal, the most ancient and primitive form of excitement. So too however the excitement of great desires, strong feelings; the rapture of the feast, of the fight, of brave exploits, of victory, of extreme agitation; the rapture of cruelty, of destruction . . . and finally the rapture of the will, of a will heavy laden and swollen."[15] A work of 1910, dionysiac in subject

15. Friedrich Nietzsche, *The Twilight of the Idols,* trans. J. Hollingdale (Harmondsworth, Middlesex: Penguin Books, 1968), pp. 71-72; quoted in Burrow, *The Crisis of Reason,* p. 240.

and style — *The Dance Around the Golden Calf* by Emil Nolde — suggests the spirit of this passage (fig. 17); since Nolde was a committed Christian, *The Dance* may also suggest the "error" implied in worship of an idol that cannot save and in a "vitalism" already marked by death.

To these experiences of physiological and psychological escape, the moneyed classes added yet another: *décadence* as a lifestyle, expressed in a cultivated aestheticism that allowed the privileged minority to taste — through art, feelings, and states of mind of other ages and classes — a kind of spiritual *voyeurisme*. J.-K. Huysmans's famous personage, the Comte des Esseintes (the main character of his 1887 novel *Àu rebours*), constructs an elegant virtual world where, without ever having to mix with common folk, he tastes all of life's sensations in aristocratic solitude.

A related refuge from modernity was art collecting and the meticulous reproduction of life on the pattern suggested by Jacob Burckhardt in *The Civilisation of the Renaissance in Italy* (1860). It was a genuine option for only a few, yet until the 1930s it remained a sort of ideal — Huysmans's aestheticism justified by the new "science" of connoisseurship. The American Bernard Berenson, who at Harvard had attended lectures by Walter Pater's disciple, Oscar Wilde, and at the end of the nineteenth century transferred to Florence, is the paradigm of this artificial escape. His villa at Settignano, with perfect gardens in the "Italian style" designed by the Englishman Harold Pinsent; his valuable collection of *fondi d'oro* and Quattrocento panel pictures; his library (with a French section, where, among other modern writers, we find Huysmans); the photo collection, at the beginning of the century almost unique in the world; the custom-made suits, made in London and changed three times a day: these were the constituent parts of a "professor," a perfect aesthete.

This movement, too, was doomed, however, for even before Berenson went to Settignano, Nietzsche had condemned the "passivity" and "effeminacy" of scholars and collectors. "What does our great

aesthetic hunger mean," he asked, "our desperate attempt to lay hold of innumerable other cultures, this longing for knowledge which consumes us, if not the loss of myth, of a mythical home of our own, of a mythic womb?"[16]

Ceaseless Flow, Incendiary Violence, People without Hands

New myths were, of course, in the making. Freud published *The Interpretation of Dreams* in 1900, and shortly thereafter the Austrian physicist Ernst Mach explained the existence of the individual as a sequence of fortuitous sensations, branding as "illusion" all claims to constant development of personality. In the same general direction, in 1907 Henri Bergson published *Creative Evolution*, with its vision of existence as incessant flow, pure unrepeatable duration; and in 1913 Proust began *A la recherche du temps perdu*. Picasso's extraordinary cubist portrait in the Albright-Knox Art Gallery in Buffalo — a woman without any stable "image," evolving, becoming (fig. 18) — and Marcel Duchamp's experiments with figures in motion are responses to these ideas.

So too is the Futurist *Manifesto*, in which Filippo Marinetti extolled "a new beauty" diametrically opposed to all that the Renaissance and its cultivators cherished: "the beauty of speed." Writing for the Paris newspaper *Figaro* in 1909, Marinetti insisted that "a racing car with its bonnet adorned with big tubes like snakes with explosive breath . . . , a roaring car, which seems to run on machine-gun fire, is more beautiful than the *Victory of Samothrace*."[17]

In their *Manifesto*, Marinetti and the other signers (Balla, Carra, Boccioni, etc.) argue that "no work without an aggressive character can be a masterpiece"

16. Friedrich Nietzsche, *The Birth of Tragedy*, trans. R. Golffing (New York, 1966); quoted in Burrow, *The Crisis of Reason*, p. 209. In Italy itself, Berenson's contemporaries the Futurists would later inveigh against "the foul gangrene of teachers, archaeologists, guides and antiquarians," claiming that "to admire an ancient painting means to pour our sensitivity into a funerary urn, instead of projecting it afar in violent spurts of creation and action."

17. Paola Cassinelli, *Futurismo* (Firenze: Giunti, 1997), p. 30.

and announced their intention "to glorify war — the only hygiene of the world — and, together with war: militarism, patriotism, destructive anarchical activity, the beautiful ideas for which one dies and contempt for women."[18] Today, after a century tragically marked by militarism, patriotism, and destructive anarchical activity, it is hard to listen to these effusions, conscious as we are that Marinetti's longing for violence was satisfied a few years later with the assassination of a prince, a world war, muddy trenches, and nerve gas. Yet Futurist art still has a kind of brassy appeal, and today, in an age poor in ideals of any sort, many remain fascinated by the Futurists' boldness, conviction, and passion:

> We want to destroy museums, libraries, academies of every kind. We shall sing of mobs excited by work, pleasure or turmoil; we shall sing of multicoloured, polyphonic tides of revolutions in modern capitals; we shall sing the quivering nocturnal fervour of docks and builder's yards lit by harsh electric moons. . . . We young, strong *futurists* want nothing to do with the past! Make way for the merry incendiaries with their burnt fingers! Here they are! Here they are! Come right in! Torch the shelves in the libraries! Divert canals to flood the museums! Oh, what joy to see the glorious old paintings float adrift torn to shreds, their bright colours extinguished in those waters! Grab picks, axes, hammers and demolish, mercilessly demolish our venerable cities![19]

Indeed, in place of the "venerable cities" of tradition, early twentieth-century *avant garde* art sought to express a new urban vision: the German Dada master Georg Grosz's *Metropolis* (fig. 19), for instance, suggests the excitement of this first generation to face trams, trolleys, and cars, neon, and the telephone — a dizzying kaleidoscope, colorful and meaningless. Compared to the "divine" orderliness of Renaissance city planning, the only "order" in this work of 1917 is that of a frenzied hedonism,

Figure 18. Pablo Picasso, *Head of a Woman* (1909)

Figure 19. Georg Grosz, *Metropolis* (1916-17)

18. Cassinelli, *Futurismo,* pp. 30-31.
19. Cassinelli, *Futurismo,* p. 31.

or perhaps the more cynical covert order we find later in Brecht's *Stadt Mahoganny* or the Fritz Lang film *Metropolis,* both of 1926. The city — which the Greeks had chosen for the exercise of liberty and Christians for brotherly love — had come to be perceived as a prison for slaves.

The most frightening image of these Weimar Republic years, again by Georg Grosz, shows the anonymity of an industrial city with, at its center, a manikin *sans* face or hands: man disabled and deprived of identity by the efficient world which others, exploiting him, have built around him (fig. 20). Here the Futurist agenda, calling for the destruction of museums, libraries, and academies, seems to have borne fruit, for the man shown can no longer admire art, read books, or create from an inner richness, being without eyes, hands, or personality.

So much of what followed — including abstraction and informal art unconcerned with the human image — developed these themes, all articulated in an inchoative way, at the least, prior to 1930. "Pop" masterpieces of the 1960s — *Drowning Girl* by Roy Lichtenstein, for instance (fig. 21) — presuppose the *gestes* of Dada painters in the 1920s and still assert that the mystery and depth of the human person is an illusion, life a cartoon, and love a banal litany dissembling the real common denominator, sex.

And where the Renaissance had presented the body's sensual beauty as expressive of spirit, now the body, even in heroic poses evoking the past, served chiefly to sell: a pragmatic application of Nietzsche's dionysiac urge.

Shipwreck, Survival, and Broken Beauty

Looking at these and innumerable other images of our time, we may wonder whether human beings, conceived in this way, can still weep. Can they feel joy? Can they look others in the face?

Noting the preference of many twentieth-century artists for abstraction, the Spanish philosopher and critic José Ortega y Gasset — in his book

Figure 20. Georg Grosz, *Manikin Without a Face or Hands* (1920)

Figure 21. Roy Lichtenstein, *Drowning Girl* (1963)

The Dehumanization of Art, published in the 1940s — asked whether enthusiasm for an art "purified" of the human image does not betray a kind of hatred, not only of past art as an expression of systems, institutions, and values considered obsolete, but of civilization *in toto.* "Is it conceivable," he wondered, "that modern Western man bears a rankling grudge against his own historical essence? Does he feel something akin to the *odium professionis* of medieval monks: that aversion, after long years of monastic discipline, against the very rules that had shaped their lives?"[20] Then he "solves" the problem in two chapters significantly entitled "Doomed to Irony" and "Art as a Thing of No Consequence."

Ortega y Gasset's words raise more questions than they answer. How can we learn to love "the essence of our historical existence" once more? How can we escape being "doomed to irony," and how can we restore to art a significant role in articulating the human image?

In an earlier text — an article written in 1932 for the centenary of Goethe's death and published in the Berlin *Neue Rundschau* in a Germany already governed by Hitler — Ortega y Gasset had suggested a solution. In centenary years, he says, rich heirs with wealth that the past has distilled may be saddened to find "a treasure of depreciated coins," because

life is, in itself and forever, shipwreck. But to be shipwrecked is not to drown. The poor human being, feeling himself sinking into the abyss, moves his arms to keep afloat. This movement of arms, which is his reaction against his own destruction, is culture — a swimming stroke. When culture is no more than this, it fulfils its function and the human being rises above his own abyss. But ten centuries of cultural continuity brings with it — among many advantages — the great disadvantage that man believes himself safe, loses the feeling of shipwreck, and his culture proceeds to burden itself with parasitic and lymphatic matter. Some

discontinuity must therefore intervene, in order that man can renew his feeling of peril, the substance of his life. All his life-saving equipment must fail, he must find nothing to cling to. Then his arms will once again move redeemingly. Consciousness of shipwreck, being the truth of life, constitutes salvation. Hence I no longer believe in any ideas except the ideas of shipwrecked men. We must call the classics before a court of shipwrecked men, to answer certain peremptory questions with reference to real life.[21]

"Consciousness of shipwreck as salvation" would be an apt description of this book and the works it discusses. For the "broken beauty" of which we speak is the beauty of beings who bear the yoke of history and mortality, but who also have wings to lift them on high, beyond the past and present toward a future dreamed of, hoped for, glimpsed intermittently, and even — in isolated, unforgotten instants — lived, felt, embraced: a future that makes sense of past and present, breaking the seventh seal and freeing us to sing the praise of God and of ourselves, of the surprise of human goodness and the gift of holiness, fashioned as we are in God's image, saved as we are by God's grace.

---

20. José Ortega y Gasset, *The Dehumanization of Art and Other Writings on Art and Culture* (New York: Doubleday, 1956), pp. 1-50, especially p. 42.

21. Ortega y Gasset, *The Dehumanization of Art,* pp. 123-27.

A COMIC VISION? NORTHERN RENAISSANCE ART AND THE HUMAN FIGURE

Lisa J. DeBoer

3

If there is a paradigmatic image for the history of Western art, it might well be the central scene of Michelangelo's (1475-1564) Sistine ceiling, *The Creation of Adam* (fig. 1). As the history of art has been written and theorized, every tenet of art that shaped our thinking about pre- and post-Renaissance painting is there; and every tenet of art that was reversed, upended, or inverted by Modernism is there. The image of the idealized (male) body is central; the artist skillfully manipulated the rules of perspective to create a believable, fictive space for this event; and the idealized bodies and the space they inhabit work together to tell us a story, the story of the original perfection and dignity of Adam. This image has come to represent the high view of humanity encompassed by Renaissance humanism, the spark of divine creativity represented by Renaissance artistry, and, by extension, the essence of the Western artistic tradition itself.

Many of us never get beyond that central scene. It is entrancing, inspiring, and deeply moving. But if we pull back from that central scene to view the rest of Michelangelo's ceiling, another perspective on the art of the West emerges, a perspective that actually requires the broader viewpoint implied by "zooming out" from *The Creation of Adam* to take in the scope of God's creation, on the one hand, and human smallness and frailty in the face of that creation, on the other. In fact, if you were to visit the Sistine Chapel and enter through the main doors, the first scene you would encounter on Michelangelo's ceiling is a far cry from the grace and amazement of *The Creation of Adam*. Rather, you would encounter an image of the drunken, naked Noah splayed on the floor of his tent in fleshy, vulnerable, and faintly ridiculous humanity (fig. 2). Traveling the length of the chapel, past *The Creation of Adam* to the last scene, you would encounter, over the altar, an unforgettable representation of the Creator dividing light from darkness (fig. 3).

Even when one places the perfect human *(The Creation of Adam)* at the center of the Western artistic tradition, an alternative tradition frames that view, emphasizing at once the vastness of the world (the creation cycle) and, in contrast, the puny, fragile, and nearly farcical scale of human action in the Noah cycle. While Michelangelo himself was not particularly interested in this alternative tradition, preferring in most of his sculptural and painted work to meditate on the storytelling power of the idealized human body, elsewhere, particularly in Northern Europe, artists were intensely drawn to the power of this alternative vision of humanity's place in the world. Alongside the theory of art that produced the anthropocentric Michelangelo (and that Michelangelo, in turn, helped reify), was another theory that emphasized the human as part of a larger created order. This tradition fostered not only different possibilities for the representation of humans but also different understandings of the very notion of what it means to create images.

Over the next few pages, I would like to consider this alternative understanding of the artist's task and explore some of the themes that emerge when representing humanity as a result of this alternative vision. Though many Northern Renaissance artists were indeed influenced by Italian theories of art that foregrounded the idealized human figure — here I am thinking of the so-called "Romanist" painters like Jan Gossart, Bernard van Orley, Jan van Scoral, and Maerten van Heemskerck, and later, of the Antwerp and Haarlem Mannerists — in the context of this exhibition it seems worthy to explore other meanings for the human figure in the art of the Western tradition. Though my focus will be largely historical, I hope that the images and ideas pique your curiosity,

Figure 1. Michelangelo, *Creation of Adam*
Sistine Chapel (1508-1512)

Figure 2. Michelangelo, *The Drunkenness of Noah*
Sistine Chapel (1508-1512)

shed light on the images in the exhibition *A Broken Beauty,* and lead you to consider the extent to which these themes are relevant for makers and viewers of art today.

The Window and the Mirror

On the surface on which I am going to paint, I draw a rectangle of whatever size I want, which I regard as an open window through which the subject to be painted is seen; and I decide how large I wish the human figures in this painting to be.

Leon Battista Alberti,
On Painting (1436)[1]

But it is in vain that one prizes one part above another, where all parts are like the most beautiful and rich noble jewels: for here it seems that everything lives and rides out of the panel. These are mirrors, mirrors, not panels.

Lucas de Heere,
"Ode to the Ghent Altarpiece" (1565)[2]

Though for most of today's artists both Alberti's and de Heere's descriptions of painting will seem terrifically antiquated, it may still be useful to attempt an imaginative exercise. Imagine you are an artist whose metaphor for painting is the Albertian window. You stand before your canvas as if it is a window frame. You've decided what your subject is (Alberti assumed it would be figural), and mentally move it left and right, up and down, in and out until just the right point of view has been achieved. You adjust the horizon to the most effective height, place your figures to achieve the proper scale, and perhaps select some striking internal framing devices. You yourself are outside the frame in masterful control of your composition.

Now imagine you are an artist whose ideal of

1. Edited and translated by Cecil Grayson (London: Phaidon Press, 1972), p. 55.
2. As translated by Walter Melion, *Shaping the Netherlandish Canon: Karel van Mander's "Schilderboek"* (Chicago: University of Chicago Press, 1991), p. 85.

painting is de Heere's mirror, where "everything lives and rides out of the panel." The mirror is already a two-dimensional surface. While you can choose to train the mirror on different aspects of the world, the horizon, scale, and content are already locked between its vertical and horizontal bounds. Every object, human or not, exists equally present to the eye on the reflective surface of the mirror. According to Lucas de Heere, this mirror is not merely a helpful imaginative device for building up painting, as is Alberti's window, but the ideal of your final product! Your demanding task is to produce an image that looks as if it faithfully transcribes the visible world onto your surface, resulting in "mirrors, mirrors, not panels." That accomplishment is precisely what Lucas de Heere was celebrating in his "Ode to the Ghent Altarpiece."

Were I to suggest, alongside Michelangelo's *Creation of Adam*, a second paradigm image for the history of Western art, it would in fact be Jan van Eyck's (c. 1370/90-1441) Ghent Altarpiece, completed in 1432, installed in the Cathedral of St. Bavo, in Ghent (figs. 4 and 5), and long considered the apogee of Northern Renaissance painting.[3] Presenting an expansive view of the new heaven and new earth, van Eyck chose to center the lower part of the composition on Christ, not as perfected incarnate human, but as the mystic Lamb, sacrificed for our salvation, and the proper object of the adoration of the universe. Surrounding the Lamb are crowds of prophets, confessors, judges, warriors, apostles, martyrs, hermits, and pilgrims. The upper panels depict God the Father, flanked by Mary and John the Baptist and crowds of music-making angels, all clothed in rich fabrics encrusted with jewels. The naked Adam and Eve, like living statues, stand in fictive niches at the extreme right and left of the upper row.

Lucas de Heere praised each part of the altar in turn: the way you can imagine Mary's lips moving as she reads, the sparkle of the jewels in the crown

Figure 3. Michelangelo, *God Separating Light from Darkness* Sistine Chapel (1508-1512)

Figure 4. Hubert and Jan van Eyck, Ghent Altarpiece (1432)

---

3. Though it is generally argued that Hubert van Eyck (d. 1426) was also active in the creation of this work, either by beginning some of the panels or by carving an elaborate gothic housing for the panels, I will follow convention and refer to the piece as by Jan van Eyck.

Figure 5. Hubert and Jan van Eyck, *The Adoration of the Lamb,* Ghent Altarpiece (1432)

Figure 6. Albrecht Altdorfer, *The Battle of Issus* (1529)

at God's feet, the individuality of the singing angels' faces, the texture of the cloth of their robes, the dignified postures of the knights and saints, the varied faces "more than three-times hundred, not one resembling another."[4] Regarding Adam, he exclaimed, "Look how terrible, and lively Adam stands. Who ever saw in paint such a fleshy body?"[5] Notably absent in de Heere's praise are comments on space, proportion, composition, or anatomy — the values of the Albertian tradition of painting. Though Michelangelo is purported to have said that Flemings painted "without reason or art, without symmetry or proportion, without skilful choice or boldness, and finally without substance or vigour,"[6] de Heere found more than enough to praise. It is the mirror-like vitality of van Eyck's images that captured his attention. Fleshiness and liveliness count more than ideal proportion or anatomical correctness.

Window. Mirror. Each produces a different notion of the painter's task. And each opens different vistas on humanity.[7]

Big World, Small People: Landscape and Genre as Ways of Reflecting on Humanity

When I look at your heavens, the work of your fingers, the moon and the stars that you have established;

4. "Van meer als drymael hondert,/Geen d'ender en ghelijckt," fol. 201v in Karel van Mander's *Schilderboek* (Haarlem: Baschier van Wesbusch, 1604), facsimile edition (Utrecht: Davaco, 1969).

5. "Siet hoe verschrickelijck, en levend Adam staet./Wie sagh gheschildert oyt soo vleeschigh een lichame?" Van Mander, *Schilderboek,* fol. 201.

6. Francisco de Hollanda, *Four Dialogues on Painting,* trans. Aubrey F. G. Bell (Oxford: Oxford University Press, 1928), pp. 15-16. These words are part of a notorious passage on Flemish painting attributed to Michelangelo by Francesco de Hollanda and published in his *Dialogues* in 1548. The passage ends with Michelangelo admitting, "Nevertheless there are countries where they paint worse than in Flanders."

7. Panofsky's famous study *Perspective as Symbolic Form* is foundational for discussions of perspective in the West. Ernst Gombrich popularized the notion of painting as mirror in the Northern Tradition, first in his essay, "Light, Form and Texture in Fifteenth Century Painting North and South of the Alps," in *The Heritage of Apelles* (London: Phaidon, 1976), pp. 19-35; and then in his widely read *Story of Art* (first published in 1950). Svetlana Alpers made fruitful use of this distinction throughout her book *The Art of Describing: Dutch Art of the Seventeenth Century* (Chicago: University of Chicago Press, 1983).

what are human beings that you are mindful of them,
mortals that you care for them?

Psalm 8:3-4

The Ghent Altarpiece, like many other works of
Northern Renaissance art, places the drama of salvation on a big stage — in this case the new heaven
and the new earth. Humans populate the scene in
abundance but are not necessarily the center of the
story. God's creative, saving actions are the center of
the story, and as mere individuals we are only the bit
players, the supporting cast. This recognition reorga-
nizes our perspective in significant ways. God's world
looms larger, and our place in it becomes smaller. In
Renaissance painting, especially in the North, this
perspective led on the one hand to an appreciation of
landscape painting as a laudable skill that emulated
God's creative activity, and on the other hand to the
development of genre painting, that is, representations of everyday humans as common, fallible, and
sometimes laughable actors on the world stage.[8]

Many works by Albrecht Altdorfer (c. 1480-1538)
demonstrate this inverted perspective in Italian
Renaissance concepts of space, scale, and human significance. Throughout his painted and printed work,
Altdorfer used the scope of land and sky to interpret
humanity. Whether in devotional paintings featuring
the holy family or saints, deep in tangled forests, or
in a large commission like *The Battle of Issus* (fig. 6),[9]
Altdorfer appreciated the power of interpreting his
subjects through setting as well as through traditional symbolism. In *The Battle of Issus,* for example,
the two protagonists, Alexander the Great and
Darius of Persia, are nearly overwhelmed by the
swirling movement of mounted troops around them,
the sweeping landscape behind them, the apocalyp-

tic sky above them, and the majestic, mysterious
cartouche dangling over them. Only the subtlest
visual cues, a slight clearing in front of the retreating
chariot of Darius and the linear pattern formed by
a line of charging horses following Alexander, lead
your eye to the main human actors in this scene. To
assure viewers that they had indeed correctly identified Alexander and Darius, Altdorfer even wrote their
names on their shields!

While Alexander and Darius may cut small figures
in this image, the earth and sky help us understand
their significance. For Western historians, Alexander's defeat of Darius near the Syrian border marked
the end of the Persian threat to Anatolia and to the
eastern portions of the Greek/Macedonian Empire.
For the residents of the Bavarian city of Regensburg,
for whom this image was painted, Alexander's defeat
of Darius echoed the hoped-for defeat of the Otto-
man Turks who were in that very year, 1529, threat-
ening to conquer Vienna, the lynchpin of the West's
defenses against the Turks. The landscape in the
painting, which has been interpreted as an imaginative map of the eastern Mediterranean, and the
viewer's omniscient perspective on it, combined with
the astrological portents in the sky (the faint cres-
cent moon in the upper left corner contrasted to the
brilliant colors of the western sun on the right), lead
to an understanding of this battle as cosmic in scale
and consequence, far outstripping the importance of
individual human actors whose labors are caught up
in much larger patterns of significance.[10]

Less elevated but equally expansive is Pieter
Bruegel's (c. 1525-1569) interpretation of human
activity, some thirty years later, displayed in a series
of panels that show the seasons and labors of the
year.[11] Originating from late medieval traditions
that represented the months of the year with their

8. Though Wolfgang Stechow's classic study *Dutch Landscape
Painting* (London: Phaidon, 1966) did not pay a great deal of attention
to the significance of figures in landscapes, his analysis of the varied
structures and viewing possibilities of landscapes anticipated in some
ways arguments for the significance of landscape presented by Walter
Melion in *Shaping the Netherlandish Canon* and by Hans Belting in
Hieronymus Bosch, "Garden of Earthly Delights" (Munich, London, New
York: Prestel Verlag, 2002).

9. This painting was also known as *The Battle of Alexander* after its
German title *Alexanderschlact.*

10. Larry Silver, "Nature and Nature's God: Landscape and Cosmos of Albrecht Altdorfer," *Art Bulletin* 81 (Spring 1999): 194-214.

11. Five panels have been assigned to this cycle, and just exactly
how they represent the months or seasons of the year has been the
subject of much discussion. *Headlong,* the 1999 novel by Michael Frayn,
and Inge Herold's *Pieter Bruegel: Die Jahreszeiten* (Munich, London,
New York: Prestel, 2002) are two of the recent entries into the discussion. There is general agreement, however, that the five panels are part
of a cycle representing the changing seasons and tasks of the year.

Figure 7. Pieter Bruegel the Elder, *The Harvesters* (ca. 1565)

Figure 8. Hieronymus Bosch, *Seven Deadly Sins and Four Last Things* (ca. 1480-1490)

characteristic labors, these panels also imagine human activity as part of a larger, ordered cosmos. In viewing *The Harvesters* (fig. 7), for example, the viewer's eye, enjoying once again a privileged bird's-eye perspective, is drawn first to the lower right, with its group of resting, lunching harvesters. It is a convivial group. Men and women sit beneath a pear tree on bundles of harvested grain, sharing a simple meal of porridge, bread, and drink. The artist's placement of one figure, the man sprawled in sleep to the left of the group, leads the eye into the picture, over sun-ripened, golden fields where workers still scythe and bundle the grain. Continuing to the left, the eye follows a path through the field where two women carry bundled shocks of wheat to a lower meadow to dry in the sun. Further along their road, a laden wagon rolls toward the village with its abundant load. In a green field near the village, figures, now tiny and distant, take refuge from the mid-day heat in a pond. Beyond the village, the grey-green horizon with its harbor and vistas gradually bring the eye up and back to the right, past a church, where we are pulled once again into the foreground scene of gathering and resting. Work and rest, gathering and storing, male and female, humans and the land are all swept into a cyclical, dynamic, organic composition. In each of these panels and in the cycle as a whole, humans do not stand over or above the movements of nature but are imagined as a part of the order of the world.

Although I've discussed only two examples, more images could easily be proffered for the so-called "world-landscape" of Northern European painting, in which the significance of the human is interpreted in light of a large and cosmic setting.[12] I'd like to turn now from the wide-angle view to the detailed close-up. Just as the idea of painting as a mirror of

12. Walter S. Gibson, *Mirror of the Earth: The World Landscape in Sixteenth-Century Flemish Painting* (Princeton: Princeton University Press, 1989). Landscape as a visualization of our life's pilgrimage, for example, was also a prominent theme in Northern European painting. See, for example, Reindert Falkenburg's *Joachim Patinir: Landscape as an Image of the Pilgrimage of Life* (Amsterdam and Philadelphia: J. Benjamins, 1988). Catherine Levesque argues that this theme survived in varied guises well into the seventeenth century; see her *Journey through Landscape in Seventeenth-Century Holland* (University Park, PA: Pennsylvania State University Press, 1988).

the world encouraged artists to represent humans in the large setting of the land, it also encouraged artists to represent un-idealized and fallible human beings — the ugly as well as the beautiful, the foolish as well as the wise. We move then from landscape to another mode of painting that flourished in Northern Europe: genre.

The roots of genre painting are even more elusive than those of landscape. Though the word did not even appear as a critical category until the eighteenth century, images depicting common people or everyday life began to proliferate in manuscript imagery around the turn of the fifteenth century.[13] By the sixteenth century, paintings and prints offered a wide range of figural work purporting to represent humans in all their variety, at work and at play, as lovely and ugly, as saints and sinners.

One of the most striking and early uses of genre scenes in Western painting appears in Hieronymus Bosch's (c. 1450-1516) *Seven Deadly Sins and Four Last Things* (fig. 8), a painting that not only turns to everyday life to interpret its subject, but in its format represents the idea of picture-as-mirror — in this case a mirror of the eye of God who surveys the depravity of humankind.[14] The words of Nicholas de Cusa capture this picture well: "Lord . . . thou art an eye . . . wherefore in thyself thou dost observe all things . . . thy sight being an eye or living mirror seeth all things in thyself . . . thine Eye, Lord, reacheth to all things."[15] The center, source, and telos of this image is the risen but irrevocably wounded Christ, who forms the pupil of God's eye. Encircling Christ is an all-too-human spectacle of sin.

Bosch, like Bruegel, draws on an essentially

medieval taxonomy for his image — in this case, the seven deadly sins (pride, envy, anger, sloth, avarice, gluttony, lust). But rather than choosing to represent them in the traditional way, as personifications, Bosch chooses to show us these sins as genre scenes, as episodes from daily human experience, inserting familiar proverbs and humorous vignettes into each depiction to increase the immediacy of its effect.[16] The three sins conventionally considered the most dangerous to one's spiritual health appear directly below the Christ figure, aligned with the inscription "Beware, beware. God sees." Two brawling men, armed with knives and hurling chairs and tables at one another, are anger in action. In the scene to the right, a woman in an expensively appointed Flemish interior pridefully admires her reflection in a mirror. On the other side of anger, envy plays out its course as one man desires another's stylish clothing, a second man covets a woman who is literally out of reach, and at their feet a dog in possession of two tasty bones snarls at another that approaches to investigate. These are sins we can recognize — everyday, trivial, pedestrian.

Pieter Bruegel, whose early imitations of Hieronymus Bosch earned him the nickname "Droll Pieter," further developed the tradition of genre painting, though with a somewhat gentler, more sympathetic touch.[17] Where Bosch's *Seven Deadly Sins* is strongly tied to the metaphor of the mirror, Bruegel was admired for his ability to observe closely and then accurately "counterfeit" the world around him.

13. Wolfgang Stechow and Christopher Comer, "The History of the Term 'Genre,'" *Allen Memorial Art Museum Bulletin* 33, no. 2 (1975-76): 89-94.

14. Both dating and attribution for this work have been disputed. It is generally dated between 1480 and 1490 and ascribed either to Bosch himself or to his workshop. Walter S. Gibson first discussed this piece as an image of a God's-eye view of human sin in "Hieronymus Bosch and the Mirror of Man: The Authorship and Iconography of the Tabletop of the Seven Deadly Sins," *Oud Holland* 87 (1973): 205-26. See also his *Hieronymus Bosch* (London: Thames and Hudson, 1973).

15. *De visione Dei* (1453), quoted in Laurinda Dixon, *Bosch* (London: Phaidon, 2003), p. 45.

16. Dirk Bax has issued a number of publications investigating the proverbial and literary elements in Bosch's works. In English, see his *Hieronymus Bosch: His Picture-Writing Deciphered*, trans. M. A. Bax-Botha (Rotterdam: A. A. Balkema, 1979).

17. Scholars still debate the intent of Bruegel's work. One tradition views the overall direction of Bruegel's work as a satirical indictment of the lower classes resulting from increasing class stratification in the Spanish Netherlands. Though a minority opinion, this interpretive tradition is well represented by Margaret Sullivan's *Bruegel's Peasants: Art and Audience in the Northern Renaissance* (Cambridge: Cambridge University Press, 1994). Walter Gibson's extensive work on Bruegel interprets his work as more sympathetic and gently humorous, and equally indebted to native pictorial and folk traditions as to humanist sources. For a recent summary of interpretations of Bruegel's work that pays close attention to Bruegel's own social relationships, see Perez Zagorin's "Looking for Pieter Bruegel," *Journal of the History of Ideas* 64 (January 2003): 73-96.

Figure 9. Pieter Bruegel the Elder, *The Peasants' Wedding* (ca. 1566)

Figure 10. Pieter Bruegel the Elder, *The Wedding Dance* (ca. 1566)

Abraham Ortelius, who recorded the only contemporary observation on Bruegel's art, praised his ability to imitate nature.[18] A generation later, Karel van Mander claimed that during his travels through the Alps Bruegel swallowed the alpine landscape whole, only to "regurgitate" it directly onto canvas. Van Mander also believed that, in order to achieve his accurate depictions of the life around him, Bruegel went out in disguise so that he could closely examine the details of daily life — dress, movements, and customs.[19] For van Mander, Hieronymus Bosch's "droll" art was transformed by Bruegel into lively images that were witty and funny, and could provoke the most dour, straitlaced person, if not to outright laughter, at least to a smile.[20]

Near the end of his career, Bruegel painted three large panels depicting rural festivities, celebrated now for their ethnographic attention to the details of sixteenth-century Flemish rural life. *The Kermis, The Peasants' Wedding* (fig. 9), and *The Wedding Dance* (fig. 10) were probably done in the mid to late years of the 1560s, and they take peasant festivity as their theme. In the *Wedding Feast,* Bruegel invites us into a spacious barn, where stacked, harvested wheat forms a warm backdrop to a crowded feast scene. Against the wall of wheat, the bride sits at a long, crowded table, honored by the blue cloth hung behind her and the bride's crown dangling from above. To her right and left, hungry guests feast on a traditional wedding dish, keeping the servers busy as they pass out laden plates from a large, makeshift tray. Across the table, one of the musicians takes a break from piping to look longingly at the food being served to the guests. In the left foreground, a man dressed in black — very likely the groom — pours ale into enormous mugs, and above him a boisterous crowd jams the doorway. In the *Wedding Dance,* the action has moved outside, where animated pairs of dancers with stomping feet and swinging arms swirl

18. The *Album Amicorum* of Abraham Ortelius is in Pembroke College, Cambridge, and is discussed in Melion, *Shaping the Netherlandish Canon,* pp. 177-78.

19. Van Mander, *Schilderboek,* fol. 233.

20. The terms van Mander uses to describe the humorous character of Bruegel's work are *drol, gheestig,* and *cluchtigh.*

through the space. Spinning, twirling, embracing, and kissing, ample, buxom women, and men with prominent codpieces draw the viewer's eye in and out of the pictorial space. Along the way, one notes guests deep in conversation, others indulging in more food and ale, lovers embracing, and one or two men relieving themselves against a tree.

Scholars are divided on the question of how to understand Bruegel's intent in such works. Should we interpret Bruegel's genre scenes along the lines of Bosch's *Seven Deadly Sins* and recognize in these feasting and dancing peasants the sins of gluttony and lust?[21] Was Bruegel acting as an elitist urbanite condemning the failings of the lower classes — engaging in "satire at its most defamatory"? Perhaps these images are satire of a gentler sort, "universal and philosophical, addressing fundamental and enduring problems of human existence."[22] Or are the images not satirical at all, but rather comic, in which case the intent is not to laugh at, but to laugh with, to enjoy "the bond of human sympathy framed in laughter at our common human lot"?[23] Whatever position one takes on this question, all of the interpretations hinge on the close-up view of imperfect, un-idealized humans living in a very immediate, recognizable world.

Both satire and comedy, as terms borrowed from the literary sphere, are considered realist modes.[24] If they are to achieve their goals of social critique or social consolidation, they require a world we recognize and consider our own. It is appropriate at this point to note that *claims* for realism, whether literary or pictorial, and *actual* realism are not the same thing. I am not arguing here that any of these images are in fact impartial, documentary images. I am

arguing, however, that the claim of realism is present, powerful, and necessary in this particular vein of Western art.[25] Genre painters in Northern Europe continued to play on the comic potential of "realistic" genre painting well into the seventeenth century. The most famous practitioner of this art is probably Jan Steen (1626-1679).[26]

"It is the mark of true comedy that one knows how to depict and imitate everything equally naturally, both sadness and joy, composure and rage — in a word all the bodily movements and facial expressions that spring from the many impulses of the spirit." So begins Arnold Houbraken's *Life of Jan Steen* in his 1721 collection of artists' biographies.[27] Houbraken's emphasis on the imitative prowess of Steen connects his comedy to that of Bruegel. And just as Bruegel began his career imitating Hieronymus Bosch, some of Steen's early works imitate those of Bruegel, allowing Steen to align himself firmly with the by-now recognizable Netherlandish tradition of "droll," "witty," and "farcical" painters.

For most viewers familiar with the art of Jan Steen, his rowdy family scenes come first to mind. In a genre painting like *As the Old Sing, So Pipe the Young* (fig. 11), a wealth of local detail and the proverbial title inscribed in the piece present us with an image that jovially accuses the adults in this household, both parents and grandparents, of dereliction of duty. Steen sets the tone for the image by foregrounding the lavishly dressed woman at the left side of the table who slouches back in her chair, one

21. E. Scheyer, "The Wedding Dance by Pieter Bruegel the Elder in the Detroit Institute of Arts: Its Relations and Derivations," *Art Quarterly* 28 (1965): 167-93.

22. The quoted descriptions of satire are from Sullivan, *Bruegel's Peasants*, p. 98. Sullivan emphasizes the more philosophical kind of satire in these images, believing that Bruegel and his audience, while concerned about behaviors they associated with the peasantry, did not see themselves as entirely without fault as well.

23. Svetlana Alpers, "Realism as a Comic Mode: Low-life Painting Seen through Bredero's Eyes," *Simiolus* 8 (1975-76): 136.

24. See especially Sullivan, *Bruegel's Peasants*, pp. 98-126, and 115-44.

25. The extent to which fifteenth-, sixteenth- and seventeenth-century thinkers and painters distinguished between claim and fact is still a matter of debate. See *Looking at Seventeenth-Century Dutch Art: Realism Reconsidered,* ed. Wayne Franits (Cambridge: Cambridge University Press, 1997).

26. For recent work on comedy and laughter in Northern Europe, see Johan Verberckmoes, *Laughter, Jestbooks and Society in the Spanish Netherlands* (New York: St. Martin's Press, 1999); and Mariët Westerman, *The Amusements of Jan Steen: Comic Painting in the Seventeenth Century* (Zwolle: Waanders, 1997).

27. Translated by Michael Hoyle, in *Jan Steen: Painter and Storyteller,* ed. H. Perry Chapman, Wouter Th. Kloek, and Arthur K. Wheelock (Washington, DC: National Gallery of Art, 1996), p. 93. The tropes and topoi at work in Houbraken's life of Steen, as well as thorough discussions of the earlier literature on this subject, have been extensively analyzed by Chapman, "Persona and Myth in Houbraken's Life of Jan Steen," *Art Bulletin* 75 (1993): 135-50; and in Westerman, *The Amusements of Jan Steen.*

Figure 11. Jan Steen, *The Happy Company (As the Old Sing, So Pipe the Young)* (ca. 1665)

Figure 12. Jan Steen, *Marriage at Cana* (1676)

foot comfortably perched on a footwarmer and one arm extended for a refill of her wineglass. The parrot above her reminds us of how easily the young "parrot" the actions of others around them. The father and mother in this scene are seated behind the table — the mother with her baby, whose sleep temporarily shields her from the bad influence of her surroundings, and the father, who is actively encouraging bad behavior by offering his son a sample from his pipe. Behind them, an older son plays a bagpipe. The children are "piping" indeed, tobacco pipes and bagpipes, both subject to questionable associations for the seventeenth-century Dutch. The older generation is not much better. The grandfather in the corner of the room wears the *kraamherenmuts* that should be worn by the father in celebration of his child, and the grandmother, squinting though spectacles, is more intent on the lyrics of the song, which also provide the title of the piece, than on tempering the antics around her.[28]

Fascinatingly, Steen often indicts himself and his own family in such compositions. His features are those of the father in this painting. The luxurious wine-drinking woman in the foreground is a likeness of his first wife. The children, too, may very well be Steen's own son and daughter. Based on images like this, Arnold Houbraken found it easy to interpret Steen's works: "his paintings are like his way of life and his way of life like his paintings."[29] Steen's use of himself and his family may have played an important rhetorical role in his comic paintings, at once inviting the viewer into the picture and underscoring the "reality" of a scene in which he was present. Equally importantly, they also remind us of the degree to which we are all tempted and have all sinned, and that "to err is human, to forgive, divine."[30]

28. This discussion is based on H. Perry Chapman's catalogue entry for this painting in *Jan Steen: Painter and Storyteller,* pp. 172-75.

29. Houbraken, quoted in Chapman's catalogue entry for this painting in *Jan Steen: Painter and Storyteller,* pp. 172-75.

30. See Chapman, *Jan Steen: Painter and Storyteller,* p. 174, for a discussion of these ideas in the context of nature/nurture debates of the day.

Christian Vision, Comic Vision

The Spirit and the Bride say, "Come."
And let everyone who hears say, "Come."
And let everyone who is thirsty come.
Let anyone who wishes take the water of life as a gift.

Revelation 22:17

The art of Jan Steen is a far cry from Michelangelo's *Creation of Adam,* with which we began, but that is where our journey into this alternative Western tradition has taken us. The understanding of "realism" that developed in Northern Europe, manifested by the metaphor of painting-as-mirror, proved useful for both a wide-angle (landscape) perspective on humanity and for close-up (genre) scenes of daily human failings and foibles. The resulting vision of humanity is smaller rather than larger, humble rather than noble.

In its classic Aristotelian definition, this trajectory would be described as comedic. Comedy for Aristotle and for most theorists after him focuses on the average rather than the elevated; it is characterized by use of vernacular, even "realistic" diction and style rather than elite forms, playful handling of words and images, and a happy ending — often a marriage feast. Northrop Frye describes comedy as a U-shaped story, "with action sinking into deep and often potentially tragic complications, and then suddenly turning upward into a happy ending." Tragedy is only "an episode in that larger scheme of redemption and resurrection."[31] It is in this sense that Dante's great visionary work on heaven, hell, and everything in between came to be known as *The Divine Comedy.* And it is in this sense that the Bible testifies to the overall comic structure of salvation history: through God's divine providence our small, vulgar, and sinful selves are led to recognize Christ,

31. These excerpts from Frye are discussed in J. William Whedbee's *The Bible and the Comic Vision* (Cambridge: Cambridge University Press, 1998). The quotations themselves are from Frye's *Fables of Identity: Studies in Poetic Mythology* (New York: Harcourt, Brace & World, 1963), p. 25; and "The Argument of Comedy," in *Theories of Comedy,* ed. Paul Lauter (Garden City, NY: Doubleday, 1964), p. 455.

are redeemed through the momentary tragedy of his death, and are invited to a final wedding feast. We can afford to acknowledge our smallness — we can sustain corrective satire and even indulge in sympathetic laughter — because we know there is a happy ending.

In this overarching comic framework, representations of the unrecognized "God with us," of Christ incarnate, take on new resonances. Jan Steen, for instance, not only painted the comedy of daily life but also recognized that some biblical subjects lent themselves to his boisterous style — the wedding at Cana (fig. 12), for example, a subject he treated at least six times over the course of his career. In the version at the Norton Simon Museum in Pasadena, Steen presents us with his usual chaotic, crowded scene. Some figures are dressed in biblical garb; others are in seventeenth-century dress. The wedding party is seated at a table at the right, marked by more elaborate versions of the cloth back-drop and bridal crown that identified Bruegel's peasant bride. The steward of the feast stands before them, proffering a flute of the newly created vintage. One man seated at the head table starts up and looks across the room toward Christ. He appears to be one of a few people who have grasped the fact that a miracle has just taken place. Christ himself is nearly lost in the crowd; only a small halo identifies him as the worker of this wonder. In the foreground a man (who bears Steen's features) and a woman prepare to take their leave, ignorant of what has just happened, unaware of Christ's presence at this feast. Perhaps they will stay, now that a servant has extended a glass of the new wine to them. At the very left edge of the picture, cast into a shadow, a statue of Moses reminds us that the old covenant is over and the new has begun because God is with us, whether we recognize him or not.

Bruegel also explored how the Incarnation resonates differently when inserted into a "world-landscape" in his celebrated *Way to Calvary* (fig. 13). Whereas it is one thing to position ordinary humans as small bit players within a larger natural order, it is another matter altogether to recognize Christ when

Figure 13. Pieter Bruegel the Elder, *The Way to Calvary* (ca. 1564)

he is confined within our limits. Here, he is one small figure among hundreds. The teeming masses, as at the wedding at Cana, are ignorant that God is with them. For most, this is one more spectacle to enliven an otherwise ordinary week. Though we know Christ's significance, we can barely pick him out. In few other images is it so clear what it meant for Christ to take on flesh and to dwell among us.

Finally, representing the ultimate comic inversion, the most "tragic episode in the larger scheme of redemption," are images like Hieronymus Bosch's *Christ Mocked (The Crowning with Thorns)* (fig. 14). Here, we are not merely ignorant of Christ's presence; we openly mock him. The four figures surrounding Christ are representative of all humanity,[32] and as ignorant, sinful humans they misdirect their laughter, not at their own failings, but at the sinless incarnate God who looks calmly and quietly out of the picture at us. This is the same Christ, the second Adam, who chose to submit himself to the confines of nature and become small, lost in the crowd as a common criminal. This is the same Christ who dwelt with simple people who enjoyed the wedding wine without understanding its significance. This is the same Christ who gazed out from the center of the *Seven Deadly Sins,* surrounded by images of human corruption. And this is the same Christ who willingly left the joys of heaven to become the Mystic Lamb, sacrificed so that all could join the feast.

Whether centering on average humans or revealing the one perfect human in his earthly setting, a comic vision of humanity — represented here by work that embraces the smallness of humankind and the realism of human sin and imperfection, but that nonetheless holds out hope for a joyous consummation — is as much a part of the tradition of Western art as the more familiar classicizing, idealizing tradition. It remains to be seen whether there is still a place for this aspect of the Western tradition in the art of the modern world.

I would not be the first to suggest that the formalist rigors of twentieth-century abstraction, with

32. Dixon, *Bosch,* pp. 129-31.

their emphasis on the immanent potential of surface and medium and on the (supposed) independence of works of art from their larger social contexts, are an extension of the Classicist theories of art first articulated in the Renaissance and then encoded in the early modern academies. It is not outrageous to suggest that Polykleitos's *Spearbearer* in ancient Greece and Piet Mondrian's geometric abstractions in the twentieth century share a deep conviction that the production of ideal forms is the ultimate call of the artist. This historical trajectory, which dominated the telling of Western art history until the 1960s, does not leave much room for imagery that requires a less idealized realism, a less heroic sense of the human story. Even after the collapse of the Modernist consensus in the 1960s and 1970s, there has been surprisingly little room in the critical mainstream for a non-ironic, warmly human, not to mention figural, vein in art. It is an interesting challenge to consider which twentieth-century artists might offer a comic vision of humanity in their art. It is equally interesting to ponder how such artists have fared in the art world.

As just one example of the challenge of sustaining a comic tradition in the twentieth century, I would like to consider the fate of Duane Hanson (1925-1996), whose realistically painted fiberglass figures of profoundly average Americans may be construed as offering a comic vision (fig. 15).[33] Though Hanson belonged to the same generation as George Segal (1924-2000) and Edward Keinholz (1927-1994), his works did not receive much public attention until the advent of pop art in the sixties, and especially photorealism in the seventies, both of which afforded him a broader artistic context. But even then, like the photorealists with whom he is so often compared, his lifelike sculptures earned him popular admiration but little critical success.

Even after a spate of recent exhibitions, Hanson's

Figure 14. Hieronymus Bosch, *Christ Mocked (The Crowning with Thorns)* (ca. 1479 or later)

---

33. As with Bruegel, critics respond to Hanson's work differently. Some view his images of average people as "cruel caricatures," while others see the work as more sympathetic. All acknowledge that his early works from the 1960s are more violent and confrontational than his works from the seventies and eighties.

Figure 15. Duane Hanson, *Tourists* (1970)

critical fortunes have remained tenuous. While some critics are reevaluating his work, a substantial number continue to see him as an amusing but essentially trivial player in the modern art world. As Richard Dorment, the art critic for the London *Daily Telegraph,* has explained: "I can't imagine how anyone could fail to be entertained by Hanson's work. It is when you try to evaluate how important an artist he was that you run into disagreements, and these have their roots in the history of art. . . . [F]or modernist critics, illusionist art that deliberately excludes imagination and does its best to minimize expression is not art at all, but craft."[34] According to Michael Kimmelman, writing in the *New York Times,* "Magic is precisely what Mr. Hanson's sculptures lack . . . and what the works of younger artists who depict the human body, like Mr. [Charles] Ray and Mr. [Robert] Gober and Ms. [Kiki] Smith, do have. Magic, a poetic sense of the absurd and the bizarre."[35]

Assuming that realist work is lacking in imagination — or as Kimmelman would say, "magic" — echoes Michelangelo's Classicist condemnation of Flemish painting, or even Eugene Fromentin's backhanded compliment to the seventeenth-century Dutch: "Holland has not imagined anything, but it has painted miraculously well."[36] Interestingly, other critics have come to appreciate the potential meaning in highly crafted, apparently "realistic" work such as Hanson's. For critic Roberta Smith, comparisons to Charles Ray, Robert Gober, and Kiki Smith miss the point:

> His work hardly presages the figurative sculpture of the 90's, which almost invariably represents the body fragmented or truncated, disturbingly distorted in form or scale. . . . Hanson viewed the figure as whole and inviolate, something to be respectfully replicated

34. Dorment's reviews are available on-line courtesy of www.theartnewspaper.com. This citation was taken from his review posted on 9 April 1997 and available at http://www.theartnewspaper.com/artcritic/level1/reviewarchive/archive1.html.
35. Michael Kimmelman, "Is Duane Hanson the Phidias of Our Time?" *New York Times,* 27 February 1994, sec. 2, p. 39.
36. Eugene Fromentin, *Masters of Past Time: Dutch Painting from Van Eyck to Rembrandt,* ed. H. Gerson and A. Boyle (Ithaca, NY: Cornell University Press, 1981), section XI.

down to the last detail and presented as is, in all its everyday ordinariness. The most affecting quality of his art may simply be his own careful attention to his figures' painted surfaces and telling details. It balances the brutal honesty of his approach with a tenderness that is reverential, sweet and self-effacing.[37]

Elsewhere in her review, Smith makes an explicit connection between Hanson and the "centuries-long tradition of meticulous, devotional verisimilitude that began in Northern Europe in the 15th century." She sees in Hanson's art a vital link to this earlier tradition in Western art, this alternative tradition, which gently exposed human failings by attending to the smallness of our everyday humanity in a vast and complex world.

Duane Hanson is only one artist who might be taken as a contemporary representative of a comic vision in Western art, and I would not want to suggest that his hyper-realism is the only appropriate style for the expression of such a vision. Nonetheless, I do think it notable that critics, both sympathetic and not, recognize in his detailed treatment of quotidian subjects a wholeness and engagement that sits equally uncomfortably in the classical tradition as in our more alienated, dyspeptic age. I've asked artist and art historian friends to think of other artists who might represent the survival of a "comic vein" in the twentieth century. Though we were able to propose a number of possibilities, most, like Duane Hanson, do not fit neatly within the critical categories at play in the art world.

All of which poses a nagging question: have we in the visual arts tacitly rejected the comic vision as an important perspective on our own world? Is it possible, or even desirable, to resurrect this vision for our own age? Perhaps the task is not as utopian as it might seem. In the art world, though we may now be too distant from *The Creation of Adam* — from an age where the idea of an ideal human, in some imagined prelapsarian beauty, could be thought uni-

versally meaningful — we still do, in fact, find the human body a bearer of meaning, however partial, truncated, and distorted it might be. A return to the comic vein in Western art would not be a return to Adam but a return to Noah. Faintly ridiculous, naked, and drunk in his tent, Noah is not perfect, but neither is he partial. He is, rather, human — one small, fallible part of a much larger story that began with the separation of light and darkness and will end with a heavenly feast. In reclaiming the figure in Western art, Adam may be a part of our past. But Noah may offer hope for our future.

37. Roberta Smith, "Tenderly Replicating the Banal," *New York Times,* 18 December 1998, sec. E, part 2, p. 37.

Mary McCleary, *I fled him down the days and down the nights* (2000)

BEAUTY LOST, BEAUTY FOUND: ONE HUNDRED YEARS OF ATTITUDES

Gordon Fuglie

4

There is something crazy about a culture in which the value of beauty becomes controversial. It is crazy not to celebrate whatever reconciles us to life.

PETER SCHJELDAHL[1]

New York critic Peter Schjeldahl writes from within the art world — or, more accurately, The Art World, that cluster of institutions, artists, and their public that go to galleries and museums, make or purchase certain kinds of art, or enroll or teach in the numerous college fine art programs in North America. Starting around 1990 and continuing into the present, Schjeldahl, along with a few critics and curators within The Art World, began to notice the prolonged absence of beauty in modern and contemporary art and concluded that something was amiss.

One of the first epiphanies of awareness of the absence of beauty came to art critic Dave Hickey in the late 1980s. He was participating in one of those perpetual panel discussions titled "What's Happening Now in The Art World." As he was daydreaming and plotting a brisk departure to the parking lot as the discussion wound down, a question from the audience about "The Issue of the Nineties" penetrated Hickey's reverie. For some reason still unknown to him, he snapped to attention and heard himself say: "The issue of the Nineties will be beauty." The audience stared blankly at Hickey and then began filing out of the auditorium as he launched into an impromptu, impassioned brief on the need for beauty in contemporary art.[2]

But Hickey's notion eventually proved correct. Within The Art World of the 1990s the idea of beauty flowered as the most vibrant and enduring bloom in a bouquet of other contemporary art issues, most now faded. And it persists; most aestheticians, artists, and critics are still grappling with beauty's return, groping for its defining qualities.

From the present vantage point, one cannot help but wonder what sort of entity The Art World is and how it lost its sense of beauty in the twentieth century. Aren't art and beauty, if not synonymous, at least hand-in-hand, aesthetic partners? Before I proceed, some clarification is in order. The Art World is in truth a comparatively small and elite cultural entity. It takes itself very seriously, is adequately funded if not always wealthy, and is narrowly self-defined and, as a consequence, self-referential. It is, therefore, often oblivious to artists and artistic currents beyond its confines. And because its self-reinforcing ideology is also exclusive — often mysteriously so — it appears to function like a corporation seeking to protect and maximize its market share, erecting barriers against would-be interlopers. Independent-minded art critics, like the expatriate Canadian Doug Harvey of Southern California's *L.A. Weekly,* have recognized and chronicled these behaviors of The Art World. Harvey has even given it a fitting corporate acronym, TAW, to designate its insularity. Since I find Harvey's exercise in branding very appropriate, I here advise the reader that I will use TAW to designate The Art World in this chapter and the following one.

Historically, TAW is the child of Modernism, a European movement begun in the industrializing nineteenth century that consciously broke continuity with previous aesthetic, social, and religious traditions in quest of new visions for a society in flux. In some instances Modernist artists gleefully

1. "Notes on Beauty," in *Uncontrollable Beauty: Toward a New Aesthetics,* ed. Bill Beckley (New York: Allworth Press/School of Visual Arts, 1998), p. 55. This essay originally appeared in *Art Issues* 33 (May/June 1994).

2. Dave Hickey, "Enter the Dragon," *The Invisible Dragon: Four Essays on Beauty* (Los Angeles: Art Issues Press, 1993), pp. 11-12. Hickey published a number of essays in the 1990s on beauty and its place in the contemporary art world.

Figure 1. Alphonse Mucha, *Nature* (ca. 1900)

sought to subvert the artistic legacy of the past, constituting themselves as various avant-gardes to lead art and society to a future of progress, purity, and liberation. By the early twentieth century, notions of beauty that placed pleasure and meaning in the idealized human form (especially the female form) or in celebratory, sinuous representations of the natural world — both typical of Art Nouveau (fig. 1) — were discredited by impatient, righteous Modernists. Their quest for pure and absolute forms aimed to purge art of "impure" decoration or ornament.[3] In the case of Art Nouveau, this was ironic because it, too, styled itself as modern — literally, the "new art." Increasingly, Modernists, especially in the years between the World Wars, gained the conviction that art history was on the side of innovation for its own sake, not the continuity or reworking of tradition in terms of the present.

European Modernism landed decisively on American shores with the International Exhibition of Modern Art held at New York's Sixty-ninth Regiment Armory in 1913, where some three hundred works from the Continent caused a sensation and scandal — none more than the skittering tawny cubist planes of Marcel Duchamp's painting, *Nude Descending a Staircase* (fig. 2).

Jumping forward in time, in 1960, just two generations later, Modernist ideas had won over a significant number of American artists and a growing number of prominent urban collectors and had enlisted adherents in higher education throughout North America. Modernist art — often abstract in form or expressively distorted when it was repre-

3. See Wendy Steiner, *Venus in Exile: The Rejection of Beauty in Twentieth-Century Art* (New York: The Free Press, 2001), for a centrist feminist and mainly literary critique. In its zeal to eliminate, purify, and abstract, Charles Jencks's *What Is Post-Modernism?* 4th rev. ed. (Chichester: John Wiley & Sons, 1996) wittily characterizes Modernism as an heir to the radical Protestant Reformation. Finally, was Art Nouveau an avatar of Post-Modernism? According to Paul Greenhalgh, the movement was all about "the possibilities of eclecticism," and, as such, "absorbed the sources and ideas available to it; it was to do with the assimilation, not elimination, of stimuli" and therefore "had the potential to be all-embracing and [historically] cumulative, and thus offered the best option for intervention in a changing world." Paul Greenhalgh, ed., *Art Nouveau 1890-1914* (New York: Harry N. Abrams, 2000), p. 430.

sentational at all, and increasingly produced in large formats — became the dominant contemporary art form among cultural elites. When this happened, TAW was constituted in North America. TAW absorbed Modernism's ongoing quest for the pure and the new and learned to ignore or demean all it deemed as unworthy of the quest. This development eventually meant cutting loose the general public, who experienced frustration, alienation, and anxiety in the presence of Modernist abstraction and distortion. Just as the avant-garde dismissed works of art they deemed insufficiently progressive, they also viewed the general public as an audience unworthy of the aspirations of Modernist art.

By the end of the 1960s, however, those aspects of Modernist art that its advocates held as canonical — purity of abstract form on the flat picture plane, its quest for the limitless Sublime (often at the expense of beauty), its cult of autonomous heroic masculinity, and the primacy of the subconscious — were met with growing skepticism by a newer generation of artists and critics who saw these notions as constraining, arbitrary, or, ironically, dated.

It was in this climate of shifting values that Postmodernism emerged, initially causing a flurry of anxiety within TAW, which had bet all of its chips on Modernism. Not for long, however; TAW's Modernist legacy of institutionalizing "the new" was deployed to harvest the new crop of Pop Art, Conceptual Art, Earth Art, Performance, Light and Space, Installation, Video, and mixed media photographic works, bringing them into TAW's refurbished confines. This widened the field of contemporary art, which previously had given primacy to abstract painting. University galleries and museums lined up to show this work, and a new style of museum, the "MOCA" (museum of contemporary art), was built to display the wide range of Postmodern expressions. To complete the reconsolidation of TAW under its newly raised Postmodern banner, Postmodern artists were hired as faculty (often under the "new media" category) in collegiate art departments, and critics who championed Postmodern artists and theories found willing publishers. To a degree, and as a com-

Figure 2. Marcel Duchamp, *Nude Descending a Staircase, #2* (1912)

ponent of Postmodernism's claim to multicultural fairness, feminists and "artists of color" were finally accommodated. Thus order was restored within the reconfigured precincts of TAW — at least that was the view from the inside.

The rise of the "beauty issue" twenty years later, however, caught TAW off its guard, just as the splintering multiplicity of art forms did in the late 1960s. Critics Schjeldahl and Hickey have tried to connect with this resurgent idea, though they too often engage beauty from examples culled from TAW's stable of contemporary artists. But who can fault them? With serious reflection on beauty absent from much of the American art scene for some fifty years, the resulting art historical continuity gap must be bridged before critics will broaden their horizons.

Among the most focused ruminators on beauty in the past decade is Arthur C. Danto, first an academic philosopher and later the art critic for *The Nation*. Writing from a rationalistic framework typical of the Anglo-American school of analytic philosophy, he attempted to address beauty in contemporary art throughout the 1990s.[4] Most likely it was Danto's rigorous approach and mastery of concepts (compared to non-philosopher art critics who were then hastily trying to assemble a toolbox of aesthetics) that obtained him an invitation to participate in the Hirshhorn Museum's exhibition and accompanying book *Regarding Beauty: A View from the Late Twentieth Century* in 1999.[5]

Regarding Beauty attempted to summarize ten years of TAW's discussion of the subject, back-filling the long stretch of time when beauty was marginalized. As an exhibition it offered a mixed array of examples from Modern and contemporary art as a kind of evidence of beauty's abiding presence, even while TAW had presumed it missing in action for decades.

But despite best intentions, *Regarding Beauty* — the exhibition as well as its book and symposium — proved problematic. This promising enterprise went awry mainly because it was created from within TAW, which had collaborated in beauty's dismissal in the first place. In other words, the project's organizers were not thinking just inside the box, but at its epicenter. The book is disappointing. For example, the opening essay, "The Misadventures of Beauty," by Neal Benezra, then the Hirshhorn's Assistant Director for Art and Public Programs, is a familiar summary of Modern Art with its cast of canonical artists, works, and events from TAW's own master narrative — really, little more than a conveyor-belt tour of "how beauty fell out of favor in the twentieth century." The essay by Hirshhorn's Associate Curator Olga M. Viso, entitled "Beauty and Its Dilemmas," gives a smidgeon of art history — mainly variations on the Greek Classical ideal — followed by a befogged, conflicted discussion about subjective and intangible aspects of beauty.

And then there is the work in the exhibition. A project that seeks to find beauty in the art of a period that has been silent about beauty or even hostile to it carries the promise of either an encounter with overlooked work by established TAW artists or — more exciting — the introduction of artists and works previously unknown and outside TAW. But this promise was not realized. Instead, TAW warhorses by Cindy Sherman, Yves Klein, Willem de Kooning, Pablo Picasso, Edward Ruscha, and Andy Warhol were put through their familiar paces, but now the viewer was asked to saddle them with the curators' confused notions of beauty. Ms. Viso summarizes her enterprise tellingly: "The exhibition's structure is pointedly paradoxical in that a certain amount of subjectivity was required to designate objects as 'beautiful.'"[6] Is this not the application of a personal conceptual veneer onto the original artistic and social premises of the works, a number of which, incidentally, were infused with Late Modernist irony or nihilistic notions?[7] (See figs. 3a, 3b.) Ms. Viso also

4. Arthur C. Danto, *The Abuse of Beauty: Aesthetics and the Concept of Art,* The Paul Carus Lectures 21 (Chicago and La Salle: Open Court Publishers, 2003), is a culmination of over ten years' engagement with the subject of beauty.

5. Arthur C. Danto, "Beauty for Ashes," in *Regarding Beauty: A View of the Late Twentieth Century,* ed. Neal Benezra and Olga M. Viso (Washington, DC: Smithsonian Institution, 1999), pp. 183-96.

6. Viso, "Beauty and Its Dilemmas," in *Regarding Beauty,* p. 88.

7. To name a few examples, see Janine Antoni, pp. 44-45, Andy Warhol, p. 50, and Sigmar Polke, p. 68, all in *Regarding Beauty.*

hoped that *Regarding Beauty* would encourage "the continued dialog on one of the most enigmatic and provocative concepts in human history."[8] When "beautiful" is book-ended by quotation marks and the concept is declared enigmatic instead of capable of clarity, we are alerted that the writer is distancing herself from her subject. And perhaps safely so; a courageous plunge into the history of beauty could lead to some jarring and illuminating discoveries.[9] So, too, Viso's call for more dialogue reflects Postmodern TAW's fondness for discourse and commentary without conclusion. And who are the discussants Viso and TAW will invite to this dialogue, and what outcomes are desired? For when the task is the consideration of beauty, we cannot avoid immersion into the rich legacy of our past.

With more than a brief nod to the Greeks, we also need to consider their Roman and Byzantine heirs and Medieval attitudes. We must consider Scholastic philosophy of the High Middle Ages, take up the Neo-Platonism of the Renaissance, evaluate the Kantian legacy of the Enlightenment, and rediscover Modernist understandings from the nineteenth and twentieth centuries. Indeed, if more dialogue on beauty is called for, then let us hear anew the voices of Aristotle, Plato, Pythagorus, Vitruvius, Thomas Aquinas, Leon Battista Alberti, Giordano Bruno, Immanuel Kant, John Ruskin, Benedetto Croce, Jacques Maritain, Etienne Gilson, Simone Weil, Meyer Schapiro, and, most recently, the feisty maverick Frederick Turner.[10]

8. Viso, "Beauty and Its Dilemmas," p. 88.

9. Consider the German poet Rainer Maria Rilke's notion of beauty from the first of the *Duino Elegies* published in 1923: "For beauty is no more/than the beginning of terror that we're still just able to bear,/and we admire it so, because it serenely disdains/to destroy us. Every Angel is terrifying." Further, in "Archaic Torso of Apollo," Rilke asserts that just such a powerful, terrible encounter with an ancient Greek fragment of an Apollo statue — so powerful, it aesthetically takes the measure of the viewer — results in the conclusion that "You must change your life." See *The Essential Rilke*, ed. and trans. Galway Kinnell and Hannah Liebmann (Hopewell: The Ecco Press, 1999), pp. 76-77 and pp. 32-33.

10. None of these authors was cited in Viso's essay notes in *Regarding Beauty*. Their works are readily found, excepting perhaps Schapiro and Turner. For Schapiro, see "On Perfection, Coherence, and Unity in Form and Content," in Beckley, ed., *Uncontrollable Beauty: Toward a New Aesthetics*, pp. 3-13; for Turner, see *Beauty: The Value of Values* (Charlottesville: University Press of Virginia, 1991).

Figure 3a. Janine Antoni, *Lick and Lather* (1993)

Figure 3b. Detail, single chocolate head, from Janine Antoni, *Lick and Lather*

Figure 4. Michael Kenna, *Tre Colline Vineyard, Napa Valley, California, USA* (2003)

Figure 5. Freeman Patterson, *Light in the Forest* (1995)

Figure 6. Peter Voulkos, *USA 41* (1960)

In noting how *Regarding Beauty* fell short of its promise, we will do well to remember Doug Harvey's assertion that one of TAW's major premises is based upon exclusion. That is, TAW ignores artists and works that don't fit into its self-referential and self-perpetuating realm. In fact, TAW simply continues the exclusionary practices that defined Modernist avant-gardes from the early twentieth century on. So when TAW was faced with the resurrection of beauty in the 1990s, an ideal with a long history, its curators could make sense of their project only by dealing with artists already within their compound. Therefore, when Dave Hickey wondered about the absence of beauty in the discourse of contemporary art in 1990, should we believe that beauty was in fact nonexistent in the art of North America? Only if the point of reference is TAW. Beyond its confines there is no shortage of current work with contemporary sensibilities that joins a continuum of traditional and historical understandings of beauty.

This is evident in fine art photography. Starting in the late nineteenth century, there has been a continuous tradition of landscape photography (to name one genre), as anyone who has ever hung a Sierra Club calendar in their home or office knows. To cite just a few accessible examples from our era, Michael Kenna (fig. 4) and John Sexton are masters of black and white, and the beauty in their work comes from unity of subject, artist's recognition of moment and place, composition, aesthetic capacities of light, and expertise in the darkroom. In New Brunswick, Canada, Freeman Patterson produces studies of his native land and beyond that are known for their precisely measured chromatic balances and are informed by his spiritual and environmental views (fig. 5).

In addition, there are abundant examples of beauty — classic and quirky, raw and primal — from ceramists, artists working in clay. And despite the bold, visceral work of the late Peter Voulkos (1924-2002), a "life-force" to be reckoned with who single-handedly stormed TAW's exclusionary perimeter to secure his own inclusion within, his example remains an exception (fig. 6). Ceramic art is still consigned to TAW's equivalent of apartheid Bantu-

stan — separate and unequal. Schjeldahl noted this condescension as a "hardwired prejudice in the art world [regarding ceramic art] as a minor, craftsy, retrograde medium."[11]

One of the more heartening examples of the exploration of beauty in contemporary art is in the return of figuration and representation in drawing, painting, and sculpture, the kind of work I have been studying and exhibiting for the last fifteen years. As the iron grip of Modernist strictures weakened, figuration and representation made a serious comeback in the 1980s, and by 2000 a critical mass of senior and junior artists were producing significant work. These resurgent "representationalists" are now producing compelling still-lifes, portraiture, figure studies, landscapes, and narratives — and engaging with old and new ideas about content and beauty.

In addition to the renewal of representational art, there has been a rethinking of the art history of Modernism. Bram Dijkstra's recent book *American Expressionism: Art and Social Change, 1920-1950* is a polemical overview that seeks to reclaim the status of the socially engaged, expressionist figuration that the High Modernist/Abstract Expressionist juggernaut obliterated with the onset of the Cold War. He denigrates the latter for its lack of meaningful content, corporate patronage, and propagandistic advocacy by the U.S. government.[12] Another corrective is found in a recent college survey text of American art history, *Framing America: A Social History of American Art*. Frances K. Pohl shows that even within Abstract Expressionism's New York domain, High Modernism's exclusionary practice dismissed the work of female and non-white artists and those abstractionists whose work lacked the aggressive

11. Peter Schjeldahl, in "Feats of Clay: Ken Price's Ceramic Art," *The New Yorker*, October 10, 2003, unabashedly hails Price's ceramic sculpture as "coolly, inexhaustibly beautiful," and "witty and sophisticated while shunning irony." He goes on to observe that "something . . . is afoot in the culture of art these days: a shift of emphasis . . . toward aesthetic practices that put [the viewer's] experience [of the object] first." At the close of this chapter I will describe my own experience with a recent work by Price and the apprehension of its beauty within an aesthetic informed by transcendence.

12. Bram Dijkstra, *American Expressionism: Art and Social Change, 1920-1950* (New York: Abrams, 2003).

individualism and virility that supportive East Coast critics deemed essential for inclusion in *their* avant-garde.[13] Dijkstra's and Pohl's critiques — among others — of American Modernism appear to have been emboldened equally by Postmodern skepticism about absolutist claims of universality (which critic Clement Greenberg once said could be found only in certain Abstract Expressionist painting) and the assertions that High Modernist artists made about their own work.[14] It may also be worth noting that if Dijkstra's and Pohl's critiques had appeared, say, fifteen to twenty-five years ago, TAW would have scorned them as heretical, misguided, or reactionary — as indeed happened to journalist Tom Wolfe when his prescient *The Painted Word* appeared in 1976.[15] Between then and now, however, TAW's defensive perimeter around High Modernism's canonical artists was breached, and we are beginning to enjoy a wider, more inclusive vision of North American art history.

But if TAW's defenses around its Modernist canon have eroded with a wider and deeper understanding of art history, there remains within its walls a durable barricade to repulse a very particular, reemergent tendency in Postmodern art: religiously themed work. Should an artist want to incorporate an earnest spirituality or un-ironic religious content combined with humanistic figuration, well, woe unto that artist. According to figurative painter Eric Fischl, one of the most stringent taboos in subject matter for contemporary artists is religious belief, that is, "spirituality

within religious identity."[16] Certain more ideological elements within TAW might attack an artist for this approach, but a more likely reaction when in the presence of the artist and his or her religious work is averted eyes, a hastily muttered "Your work is, uh, interesting," evasive maneuvers, and future shunning.

This prejudice against intended religious content, especially work with Judeo-Christian themes, is again a holdover from Modernism's practiced exclusions and is embedded in the secular scholarship of Modern art.[17] According to Sally M. Promey, a historian of American art, the roots of this prejudice are found in the secularization theory of modernity that embodies three contentions: "that modernization necessarily leads to religion's decline, that the secular and the religious will not co-exist in the modern world, that religion represents a pre-modern vestige of superstition."[18] Thus, with a few significant exceptions like the late Howard Finster, the prejudice against intended religious content, like the prejudice against ceramic art, is hardwired in TAW, virtually an "article of faith" within its realm.[19]

This prejudice also has negative consequences for our understanding of art history. Richard Brettell, a scholar of European Modernism, bemoans the abundance of unstudied Christian-themed art production in late nineteenth-century Symbolism, a modern movement in which the beautiful loomed

13. Frances K. Pohl, *Framing America: A Social History of Modern Art* (New York: Thames & Hudson, 2002), pp. 434-45.

14. In the early 1990s, Greenberg told the L.A. artist John Frame that what he wrote about art in the 1950s and 1960s was limited to that time and place. Frame recalls Greenberg enthusing about figurative work that he had recently seen in Canada (author's conversation with John Frame, 6 February 2004). One example of the inflated claims about the social impact of Abstract Expressionist painting comes from Barnett Newman: "[New York art critic] Harold Rosenberg challenged me to explain what one of my paintings could possibly mean to the world. My answer was that if he and others could read it properly it would mean the end of all state capitalism and totalitarianism." Quoted in Robert Hughes, *American Visions: The Epic History of Art in America* (New York: Alfred A. Knopf, 1997), p. 494.

15. Tom Wolfe, *The Painted Word* (New York: Farrar, Straus & Giroux, 1975). Witty, though rather selective in its critique of the New York art scene from 1950 to 1970, the book has remained in print for over twenty-five years.

16. Frederic Tuten, "Fischl's Italian Hours," *Art in America,* November 1996, pp. 77ff. Fischl can afford to speak out; he's been largely accepted by TAW.

17. Christopher Knight, "Overstating the Religious?" *Los Angeles Times, Calendar,* October 6, 2003, took up the role of TAW's antipathy toward intended religious content in his negative review of the methodology undergirding the exhibition *The Circle of Bliss: Buddhist Meditational Art* at the Los Angeles County Museum of Art. He accused its organizers of "proselytizing" for Tantric Buddhism because they attempted to educate museum visitors about the theology and practice of the sect that, of course, informed the patronage and production of its sacred art.

18. Sally M. Promey, "The 'Return' of Religion in the Scholarship of American Art," *Art Bulletin* 85, no. 3 (Sept. 2003): 584.

19. I am grateful to Theodore Prescott for this observation. He reminded me that Modernism's embrace of Primitivism since the early twentieth century "allows" for religious belief that fits stereotypes of the so-called authentic, natural, uneducated, naïve artist. Thus Finster (a Southern white working-class evangelical Christian) and African American and Latino artists who use religious content gain a qualified inclusion within TAW because of their exceptional status as "irrational savages," the ennobled Other.

large: "[S]pecifically religious art is the least studied arena in modern art production, mostly because the Church has been viewed by secular scholars as a traditional institution that failed to evolve in a secular or modern world."[20] Following Brettell, a broadened study of fin-de-siècle and early-twentieth-century art will show that beauty and religion were important components in Early Modern art movements, drawing on sources in pre-Modern Western art.[21]

Toward a Definition of Beauty

So, too, are beauty and religion crucial to understanding a growing body of work produced in our own time, and particularly the work of the artists in *A Broken Beauty*. In light of this, and as an alternative to the secularization theory of modernity permeating TAW, it is therefore crucial to reckon with this work in an appropriate interpretive framework. Following my many encounters with contemporary art that engages religious and spiritual themes, I realized that I needed to find modern philosophers and critics whose work in aesthetics was informed by a transcendent perspective. In philosophical language, the transcendent is that reality which is not confined to the world we see and mentally evaluate. The nontranscendent philosophical view, currently expressed by many in the Anglo-American school of analytic philosophy, takes Immanuel Kant's (1724-1804) understanding of the limitations of reason to confirm a world-immanent view of reality — that is, the only reality that humans

can know is limited to the mundane, material world. It also believes in the finality of death and no afterlife.

A transcendent reality is by definition a super-reality. Philosophers who reason from a transcendent framework often call this super-reality God, the divine being who is also the creator of the universe. Moreover, they understand humankind as a vital part, if not the crown, of God's creation. In addition, many of these philosophers believe that human beings can gain insight into the transcendent because God's creation is intelligible, marked by God's purpose and order, and that the human spirit enters into a transcendent life after death.

In my quest for a transcendent aesthetic framework for reckoning with beauty, I found a number of modern and contemporary thinkers who drew upon the Aristotelian-Thomistic tradition. This direction in philosophy was significantly revitalized in the twentieth century by the French Roman Catholic philosopher, aesthetician, and political thinker Jacques Maritain (1882-1973). Virtually no one in TAW who was drawn into the recent discussion of beauty seems aware of Maritain and his landmark contributions to aesthetics, and they likely would respond in bemusement to learn that Maritain structured *his* philosophy on a theory of beauty that was outlined in the thirteenth century by a priest and philosopher, Thomas Aquinas (1225?-1274). Aquinas's ideas, a deepening of Aristotle's (384-322 BCE) philosophy from Antiquity, now known as Thomism or Scholasticism, continue to have traction in our day, though no system aspiring to comprehensiveness that dates back eight hundred years can escape the impact of subsequent scientific and philosophical developments.[22] Nevertheless, as an overarching

---

20. Richard Brettell, *Modern Art: 1851-1929*, Oxford History of Art (New York: Oxford University Press, 1999), p. 21. Consider his challenge to scholars of Modern art: "The fascination of Symbolist artists with religious cults of many sorts and with spiritualism in general was so pervasive and such a major component of various modern movements or groups that the sacred must be placed at the center, rather than the periphery, of any study of modern representation."

21. Donald Kuspit, in "Revisiting *The Spiritual in Art*" (paper presented at Ball State University, Muncie, Indiana, January 21, 2004, available online at www.bsu.edu/web/jfillwalk/BrederKuspit/RevisitingSpiritual), demonstrates the influence of Russian Orthodox church interiors on Wassily Kandinsky's (1866-1944) abstract paintings. Like Kandinsky in the early twentieth century, Kuspit also calls for a reengagement with spiritual concerns in contemporary art.

22. Among the more vital and popular interpreters of Aquinas's aesthetics is the Italian semiotician and structuralist, Umberto Eco. See his books *The Aesthetics of Thomas Aquinas*, trans. Hugh Bredin (Cambridge, MA: Harvard University Press, 1988), and for a broader treatment, *Art and Beauty in the Middle Ages* (New Haven: Yale University Press, 1986). It should be noted that Eco, a "global Post-Modern intellectual," now distances himself from these books that he wrote in the 1950s, he says, with the zeal of a young academic believer in Aquinas's system. Nevertheless, he continues to allow some credence to the Thomist enterprise in our day. Meanwhile, Eco's succeeding "faiths," structuralism and semiotics, have had to weather mounting critiques in academia in recent years. Will Eco come full circle in his old age?

system striving to explain the universe and human-kind's place in it, Aquinas's magnificent philosophical structure was flexible enough to allow subsequent generations to develop it further.

Maritain and his contemporary, Étienne Gilson (1884-1978), were the key figures responsible for a major breakthrough in Thomist-inspired aesthetics in the twentieth century. In philosophical circles they became known as Neo-Thomists. Their writings on aesthetics and beauty, especially Maritain's signature work, *Art and Scholasticism,* influenced many important Modernist artists of the twentieth century, including the poets T. S. Eliot and Czeslaw Milosz, the American fiction writer Flannery O'Connor, and the composer Igor Stravinsky. Stravinsky's Maritain-influenced Harvard lectures, "The Poetics of Music," is only one example of the breadth and ubiquity of that influence only fifty years ago. Maritain's and Gilson's writings on aesthetics held their own in the mainstream of the art world through the 1960s, after which they fell into obscurity.[23] Late twentieth-century ironists, not surprisingly, have had little use for Neo-Thomism's convictions, including a hearty confidence in a real world and natural order interpenetrated by divine life. Even so, this scholarly and critical tradition persists in the work of the American Maritain Association and its northern counterpart, The Canadian Jacques Maritain Association, both of whom advance Neo-Thomist philosophy and aesthetics and critique contemporary culture.[24] Indeed, it is the historical con-

tinuity of this tradition in our time that attracted me to it as a methodological tool for understanding beauty.

In Neo-Thomist aesthetics, beauty is evident in the order of the universe. This order, when grasped by human reason, gives us an aperture onto the transcendent, the divine Other. Commencing with Aristotle, expanded upon by Aquinas, and further developed by Neo-Thomist philosophy in our age, the natural order of the universe is what grounds art and morality. Since the Enlightenment, however, this understanding of the natural order has been challenged by modern science and especially by the philosophical legacy of Kant. As a result, the understanding of beauty as an indicator of the transcendent was replaced by the notion that the beautiful lies only in the realm of individual human freedom and creativity. Thus the perception of beauty was limited to subjective experience and held no key to intimations of the transcendent or the natural order of the universe. Maritain, Gilson, and successive Neo-Thomists have critiqued this modern diminishment of beauty to purely subjective experience or, worse, a cultural construct in service of dominant ideologies. Their enterprise is integrative, a restoration of the transcendent to the immanent for a fuller understanding of beauty and art in human existence.

To be sure, there is much to overcome. Two hundred years of Kantian subjectivity coupled with the spurning of the beautiful by Modernist avant-gardes have left us with an impoverished language for the discussion of beauty or of aesthetics in general. Attendees at the symposium for the exhibition *Regarding Beauty* at the Hirshhorn Museum in 1999 heard a great deal of discussion about the topic of beauty by principal speaker Arthur Danto. But when pressed for a definition of beauty's characteristics, he was not willing to go beyond the TAW bromide of "you know it when you see it."[25] To risk definition

23. Readers new to Maritain may be surprised to learn that he moved comfortably among Europe's avant-garde artists, such as Pablo Picasso and Jean Cocteau. See the following works by Maritain on art and aesthetics: *Art and Scholasticism with Other Essays,* trans. J. F. Scanlan (Whitefish, MT: Kessenger, 2003); *Creative Intuition in Art and Poetry,* The A. W. Mellon Lectures in the Fine Arts (New York: Pantheon, 1953); *The Responsibility of the Artist* (New York: Scribner, 1960). The University of Notre Dame Press is publishing Maritain's collected works in English; vols. 9 and 10 will gather his writings on art and aesthetics. For Étienne Gilson, see *The Arts of the Beautiful,* French Literature Series (Normal, IL: Dalkey Archive, 2000); *Forms and Substances in the Arts,* trans. Salvatore Attanasio, French Literature Series (Normal, IL: Dalkey Archive, 2001); and *Painting and Reality,* The A. W. Mellon Lectures in the Fine Arts (New York: Pantheon, 1957).

24. For their publications and conferences, see the website: www. jacquesmaritain.org; it contains a link to the Canadian association. For a recent work applying Neo-Thomist aesthetics, see Alice Ramos, ed., *Beauty, Art and the Polis* (Washington, DC: American Maritain Association, 2000).

25. Correspondence with Dr. Adrienne Dengerink Chaplin, Philosophical Aesthetics, Institute for Christian Studies, Toronto, 14 February 2004. Dr. Chaplin attended Danto's lecture and recalled a question from the audience asking him for a definition of beauty. Danto left the questioner unsatisfied. Of the exhibition *Regarding Beauty,* Chaplin said, "it failed to make clear whether the works [of art] were either expressions or examples of works displaying beauty or comments and critiques of it — or both, resulting in an exhibition which, frankly, was a bit of a dog's breakfast [a mess]."

would take one in the direction of objective and classical conceptions, inevitably leading to systematic approaches — such as Scholasticism offers — that Modernism has shunned for at least half a century.

Meyer Schapiro and the Conditions for Beauty in Art

The late American art historian Meyer Schapiro (1904-1996) was certainly no Neo-Thomist, but this polymath and one-time medievalist was well acquainted with the Scholastic system and its aesthetic implications.[26] He was also an authority on Modern art and the contemporary art of his era. Most important, Schapiro was of that generation of art historians and critics formed by a deep immersion in the sources of Western culture, the kind of humanist education that became difficult to find in the second half of the twentieth century. Unlike many within the current constituency of TAW, Schapiro spoke with a careful certainty about beauty in works of art.[27] I cite Schapiro as an example because, as a mainstream secular art historian who *believed* in beauty and was conversant with transcendent concepts, his work complements the work of a Neo-Thomist like Maritain. He therefore provides an important parallel to transcendent aesthetic understandings of beauty. Moreover, and unlike the present situation, both Schapiro, the secular art historian, and Maritain, the Catholic philosopher, were formed in an intellectual environment in which open discussion was encouraged. And, as shall be seen, there is considerable overlap in the two scholars' conditions for beauty, as well as a fluidity of concepts between Schapiro's conditions and those of Maritain.

At the height of his career, in 1964, Schapiro gave a paper at the Institute of Philosophy in New York, entitled "On Perfection, Coherence, and the Unity of Form and Content." His purpose was to both affirm these time-honored qualities and expand on them in the Modern era. With characteristic breadth, depth, and nuance, Schapiro advanced the basic three conditions for beauty within a work of art as a whole.[28] While he did not locate these traits within a transcendent philosophical aesthetic, he did explain them in ways that parallel the aesthetic ideas of Maritain, who was Schapiro's older contemporary.

In teasing out his explanation of beauty, Schapiro was careful to add that its conditions of perfection, coherence, and the unity of form and content should not be rigidly defined by stylistic norms, like academic classicism. He advocated a supple approach that allowed for the evolving and deepening of our appreciation of a work of art through prolonged and repeated contemplation. In addition, he believed that the aesthetic richness of a work was apprehended by "collective criticism" (i.e., engagement) extending over generations. "This task is sustained by new points of view that make possible the revelation of significant features overlooked by previous observers."[29] Such an approach fosters humility in judging a work, for we can rarely see it as a whole in one encounter. We need to return to it, deepening our contemplation each time, and, as Maritain might add, deepening our delight in its presence. Moreover, Schapiro's continuity of involvement encourages a communal and temporal discovery of beauty, allowing for the impact of shifting social and cultural conditions on how we see a work from one century to the next. It discourages the once-and-for-all evaluations of self-styled tastemakers and grounds the value of a work in its ability to sustain discourse and delight across generations.

---

26. Meyer Schapiro, "On the Aesthetic Attitude in Romanesque Art," in *Romanesque Art* (New York: George Braziller, 1977), pp. 1-27. The paper originally appeared in 1947.

27. A colleague told me of attending a conference in New York in the 1980s that featured a fashionable deconstructionist. Schapiro was in the audience, and after enduring a jargon-larded theoretical presentation expressing skepticism about understanding a work of art, he remarked to those within earshot that he still believed that the task of the art historian was to get at the truth.

28. The paper was originally published in Sidney Hook, ed., *Art and Philosophy: A Symposium* (New York: New York University Press, 1966). It has been recently republished in Beckley, ed., *Uncontrollable Beauty: Toward a New Aesthetics,* pp. 3-13.

29. Schapiro, "On the Aesthetic Attitude in Romanesque Art," p. 6.

Figure 7a. Michelangelo, View of the Ceiling of the Sistine Chapel (1508-1512)

Figure 7b. Michelangelo, *The Delphic Sibyl,* Sistine Chapel (1508-1512)

In defining the conditions that constitute beauty in a work of art, I will summarize Schapiro's remarks and conclude with a discussion of beauty within the transcendent philosophical aesthetic developed by Maritain.

Perfection

The apprehension of perfection in a work of art convinces the beholder that the object embodies rightness in its makeup. In such a work this perfection means the simultaneous presence of order, integrity, and harmony. Moreover, Schapiro notes, we sense that the work *should* be this way; its appearance has a kind of inevitability to it. But he also reminds us that perfection does not rule out inconsistencies, especially in works we regard as supreme achievements. He cites the composite artistry of the Bible, the sprawling novels of Leo Tolstoy, Chartres Cathedral with its various sculptural and architectural styles, and Michelangelo's murals on the ceiling of the Sistine Chapel as inconsistent but undeniably great (figs. 7a, 7b). To these I would add the seemingly chaotic painted narrative cycles of New York artist Jerome Witkin (see fig. 9 in the following chapter). Such works are characterized by perfection in that they contain in their "incompleteness and inconsistency . . . evidences of the living process of the most serious and daring art which is rarely realized fully according to a fixed plan, but undergoes the contingencies of a prolonged effort."[30]

Coherence

We recognize coherence in a work of art when we perceive the order that the artist has created within it. A classical order is coherent because of its clear design, symmetry, and legible balance. The well-ordered whole is identifiable by a distinctness of parts, clear grouping, and definite axes. But Schapiro reminds us that there are other kinds of order possible, and our investment in a classical order will exclude the sorts of order composed of the intricate,

30. Schapiro, "On the Aesthetic Attitude in Romanesque Art," pp. 4-5.

the unstable, the fused, the scattered, and the broken. He cautions against overlooking or disregarding one kind of order because we cling to another as our model.[31] Maritain, too, allowed for a diversity of orders in Modern art as long as they were coherent within their genre.

Unity of Form and Content

For Schapiro, every shape and color is a constituting element of the content of a work; simply put, the forms make up the content. This distinguishes them from the *subject* of a work. Together the forms constitute the representation in combination "with all the ideas and feelings properly evoked by it."[32] Thus seen, the content is completed, if not yet fully apprehended, in the viewer's recognition of it.

Rather than speaking of oneness of form and content, Schapiro prefers to speak of their unity as "an accord," since the point (or points) of their conjunction is not always clear.[33] In addition, it is only after a series of encounters with works of quality that we can fully recognize a comprehensive unity that makes for a satisfactory accord. This comprehensive unity is the ground of the work's beauty. Just as he argued with regard to perfection, the once-and-for-all apprehension (the "ah-ha!," "I get it," notion) of *the* unity of form and content is beyond us, especially in complex works.[34] In these there can even be multiplicities of unities of a work's form and content. Schapiro cites again Michelangelo's mural program on the ceiling of the Sistine Chapel as an example of great complexity. Do we really believe that we can grasp the unity of its form and content in one, two, or three encounters?

Perfection, coherence, and the unity of form and content are the basic conditions for beauty in a work of art. Schapiro warns us, however, that these conditions are not to be rigidly defined by previous, singular, or narrow models. With this elemental yet flexible framework in place, we will now widen our understanding of artistic beauty through an aesthetic that encompasses transcendence.

Jacques Maritain: Beauty in a Transcendent Key

Every form is a vestige or a ray of the creative Intelligence imprinted at the heart of created being.

Jacques Maritain, "Art and Beauty" (1920)[35]

Originally written over eighty years ago, Maritain's essay "Art and Beauty" remains the standard for the discussion of beauty within a Neo-Thomist, generally transcendent framework. However, it may be used profitably from within a secular viewpoint, since Maritain did not produce it solely from a religious perspective or to serve exclusively religious ends.[36] The first sentence locates the beautiful in a reference to Aquinas: it is "that which, being seen, pleases."[37] Maritain develops this encounter with the beautiful, describing the experience as a vision gained by intuitive knowledge through the senses that leads to a delight, a rejoicing, in knowing. This is no mere knowledge; indeed, he maintains that the knowing of beauty produces "a delight which superabounds and overflows" from the act of apprehending beauty in a work of art.[38] With the constraining of beauty and the prohibition of its enjoyment under Modernism's regime, Maritain's full-blown affirmation of visual pleasure is the aesthetic equivalent of Monopoly's coveted "get-out-of-jail-free" card.

While defining beauty is important to Maritain,

35. In *Art and Scholasticism and The Frontiers of Poetry,* trans. Joseph W. Evans (New York: Charles Scribner's Sons, 1962), p. 25.

36. The essay is included in *Art and Scholasticism* (originally published in France as *Art et Scholastique* in 1920; Maritain revised the volume in 1927, with supplements, and in 1935), which was first translated into English by J. F. Scanlan as *The Philosophy of Art* in 1923. A revised version with additions, *Art and Scholasticism with Other Essays* appeared in 1949. With Maritain's approval, Joseph W. Evans produced another English translation in 1962 (cited in note 35 above). The Scanlan translation is currently published by Kessenger; see note 23 above.

37. Maritain, "Art and Beauty," p. 23. Subsequent citations are from the Evans translation. Maritain maintains that the apprehension of beauty is also an experience imbued with the good.

38. Maritain, "Art and Beauty," p. 23.

31. Schapiro, "On the Aesthetic Attitude in Romanesque Art," p. 6.
32. Schapiro, "On the Aesthetic Attitude in Romanesque Art," p. 7.
33. Schapiro, "On the Aesthetic Attitude in Romanesque Art," p. 8.
34. Schapiro, "On the Aesthetic Attitude in Romanesque Art," p. 9.

he is equally concerned to persuade his readers that the apprehension of beauty involves an *exchange* between the viewer who contemplates a work of art and the work of art as a self-sufficient whole whose preexistent beauty is "radiated" to the viewer's intellect in the act of contemplation. Maritain saw this reciprocal relationship as "that intercommunication between the inner being of things (the art object, natural vista, etc.) and the inner being of the human self which is a kind of *divination*."[39] This striking term is used to unfold the notion of beauty as transcendent; that is, beauty is beyond ordinary human understanding because it is a characteristic of the divine, and yet under certain circumstances it is capable of apprehension because creation and art's transcendent beauty is intelligible. For example, a rapt listener at a performance of Bach's *St. Matthew Passion* may experience ecstasy, a dislocation of the self, and resultant joy when certain musical and choral passages reach an accord, making for beauty; this expression and its apprehension transcends the score and instrumentation. Moreover, mystics from different religious traditions have recorded their ecstatic encounters with the transcendent — the divine — as beautiful.

For Maritain, beauty is manifested in the natural creation and in art, and "it always involves a relation to an intelligence, either God's or our own."[40] As creatures we mirror our Creator, though in a diminished glory to be sure. Yet all creatures and created things, like works of art, "are not only what they are. They ceaselessly pass beyond themselves, and give more than they have because from all sides they are permeated by the activating influx of the Prime Cause. They are better and worse than themselves, because [their] being superabounds."[41]

How different this potentially infinite understanding is from a Kantian subjectivity that locates beauty only in the mind of the viewer — that is, a work of art is beautiful merely because we think or feel it to be, not because it has beautiful characteristics in itself whether we recognize them or not.

Neo-Thomist Conditions for Beauty in Art

Aquinas listed three conditions of beauty, which Maritain identified as integrity, proportion, and radiance.[42] Together these should be understood in relation to the end of a work — that is, the order that the artist conceived in a work's attainment of its ultimate configuration.

Integrity, or Perfection
Integrity corresponds to Schapiro's notion of perfection; it was essential for Aquinas "because the intellect is pleased in the fullness of being" evident in nature and, per Maritain, in a work of art.[43] Key to Maritain's understanding of integrity was his notion of "perfection in the given case," which encouraged Modernist works that sought new precedents in art, like Futurist paintings depicting the rhythms of rapidly moving time and the simultaneity of events in urban life. Thus a dynamic, surging canvas by Umberto Boccioni (1882-1916) had integrity or perfection if it was produced in a logic that was "according to its objects and according to its ends."[44] (See fig. 8.)

Proportion, or Harmony
Proportion is the proper relation between things or parts, entailing symmetry, harmony, and balance. Proportion is essential to beauty, says Aquinas, "because the intellect is pleased in order and unity."[45] He also qualifies this condition as "*due* proportion, or harmony," denoting an accord — that is, an orderly or pleasing arrangement of parts — in nature that

---

39. Cited in John G. Trapani, Jr., "'Radiance': The Metaphysical Foundations of Maritain's Aesthetics," in *Beauty, Art and the Polis,* p. 14; emphasis added.

40. Cited in Trapani, "'Radiance': The Metaphysical Foundations of Maritain's Aesthetics," p. 14.

41. Maritain, *Creative Intuition in Art and Poetry,* p. 127.

42. Maritain, "Art and Beauty," p. 24.

43. Maritain, "Art and Beauty," p. 24.

44. Maritain, "Art and Beauty," p. 27. As an example, in Boccioni's painting of 1910, *The City Rises,* integrity or perfection would be lost in this Futurist masterpiece if the artist placed a motionless neo-classical figure in the middle of its rhythmic forms.

45. Maritain, "Art and Beauty," p. 24.

would also make for congruity in a work of art.[46]
This condition also corresponds with Schapiro's
definition of perfection that subsumes order and
harmony.

An example of new proportions and harmonies
can be found in the work of a Modernist artist whom
Maritain championed, Georges Rouault (1871-1958).
His unlikely combination of thick and dolorous
contours, a stained glass compositional sensibility
for his paintings and graphics, and crude, mannered
forms conspired to an accord of their own by being
"perfectly proportioned in their genre."[47] (See fig. 9.)
In other words, taken separately Rouault's elements
could be strange, awkward, or even ugly; but when
their forms and content were harmoniously combined, unity was the result, and per Rouault's intention, a new genre was born — a spiritual lament for
post–World War I Europe.

In contrast to Rouault, some recent figurative
paintings by Americans John Currin (fig. 10) and
Lisa Yuskavage are certainly full of unlikely combi-
nations; but they are unclear as to their motivation,
context, and meaning — not to mention willfully
disharmonious compositions and disproportion-
ate anatomical renderings. In their propensity for
extreme formulations they signify what Charles
Jencks recognized as Late Modernism's dogged
determination to overturn those traditions that
healthily link the past to the present.[48]

Radiance, or Clarity

Maritain echoes the ancient Greeks, Augustine, and
Aquinas in giving precedence to radiance, or clarity,
"because the intellect is pleased in light and intelligi-

46. Maritain, "Art and Beauty," p. 161, n. 50.
47. Maritain, "Art and Beauty," p. 27. Jacques Maritain and
William S. Lieberman's book *Georges Rouault* (New York: Abrams,
1954) was a modest publication that appeared in English, emphasizing his printmaking. Rouault scholarship tapered off at the close of
the 1970s. He is an artist well worth a fresh look in our time.
48. Jencks, *What Is Post-Modernism?* pp. 43-49; Staci Boris and
Robert Rosenblum, *John Currin* (New York: Abrams, 2003); Katy
Siegel and Lisa Yuskavage, *Lisa Yuskavage* (Philadelphia: University
of Pennsylvania Press, 2000). Beyond their formal dysfunctions,
whatever claims to art these works may have is also stifled by the
curdling sentimentality and commercial illustration sensibility that
infuses them.

Figure 8. Umberto Boccioni, *The City Rises* (1910)

Figure 9. Georges Rouault, "Nous sommes foux" (We are mad),
from *Miserere et Guerre* (ca. 1920; published 1948)

Figure 10. John Currin, *The Pink Tree* (1999)

bility."[49] This mode of apprehending beauty is knowing "the splendor of the form on the proportioned parts of matter"; or alternately, "it is a flashing of intelligence on matter intelligibly [harmoniously] arranged."[50] Maritain implies that radiance or clarity is knowable best when the mind is simultaneously relaxed and alert. By guiding our intellect to a contemplative state we set a "tripwire of anticipation" in our intellect to apprehend the integrity, harmony, and radiance that await our discovery in a work of art — or, conversely, that are found to be absent.

A Transcendent Encounter with Beauty

In conclusion, I would like to consider what happens when one applies Maritain's criteria to an actual work of art. I will describe and evaluate my experience of beauty in a ceramic sculpture by Ken Price (b. 1935), an artist based in Taos, New Mexico. The work, *Ornette* (fig. 11), from 2003, is "abstract," though its organic form suggests a broad range of associations.[51] Moreover, because *Ornette* neither represents something in the natural world nor possesses overt spiritual or religious associations, I want to demonstrate that a meaningful aesthetic experience can occur with *any* work that fulfills the conditions of beauty, not just those with overt religious content — as TAW might suspect of a Neo-Thomist approach.[52] Finally, the experience of beauty I describe with *Ornette* is a recollection of two components: my preanalytical encounter, and my subsequent aesthetic analysis of the work.

Entering the New York gallery where *Ornette* was displayed, I understood, of course, that I would be encountering works of art. I did not know, however, that new works by Price were on view; my visit was happenstance. Moreover, I had not seen any of his works in years. Glancing around the room, my eyes

49. Maritain, "Art and Beauty," p. 25.
50. Maritain, "Art and Beauty," p. 25.
51. See note 11 above.
52. All *authentic* works of art, whatever their form and content, have a spiritual dimension.

alighted on *Ornette;* its being activated the tripwire of my anticipation. Momentarily captivated, my gaze deepened on the swelling, reddish, parti-colored work, and I moved closer. At this point my senses were engaged, and, in Maritain's analogy, I drank in the "splendor of the form" radiating from the proportioned parts of the sculpture (which in this moment I was *not* experiencing *as* sculpture nor studying *as* proportions!).[53] Concurrently, I felt a connection between the inner being of *Ornette* and the inner being of my self. This was still preanalytic, and the intuition of my senses (Maritain refers to this as "intelligentiated sense") recognized in *Ornette* Price's creative intellect in the fabrication. With this recognition I found the work beautiful, and my intellect rejoiced. I also concur with Maritain who says that when the beautiful is encountered the intellect "finds itself again," or "makes contact with its own light."[54] Accompanying this perception of the beautiful, he remarks, is "that curious feeling of intellectual fullness through which we seem to be swollen with a superior knowledge of the object contemplated, and which nevertheless leaves us powerless to express it and to possess it by our ideas and make it the object of our scientific analysis."[55] Such an experience made me glad in the presence of *Ornette,* and I recall exclaiming out loud to no one but myself.[56]

Arriving at this moment, the preanalytic encounter with *Ornette's* beauty faded and I now wanted to follow my "wow" with inquiries about the work. (Who is the artist? Ken Price? *This* is a Ken Price? etc.) And this led to aesthetic analysis using the conditions of beauty described by Schapiro and Maritain.

The bulbous *Ornette* possesses integrity because it manifests a fullness of being consistent within its own genre of form. The tapering and swelling molten forms are coherent as a sculptural entity, simultaneously obeying the laws of gravity and their own viscosity. The work is proportioned accordingly,

Figure 11. Ken Price, *Ornette* (2003)

53. Maritain, "Art and Beauty," p. 25.
54. Maritain, "Art and Beauty," p. 25.
55. Maritain, "Art and Beauty," p. 164, n. 55.
56. For a similar observation, see Peter Schjeldahl, "Feats of Clay," p. 133: "One succumbs to it with a glad sigh."

twenty-one inches high and wide, I later learned, and dwells in the realm of human scale. As Peter Schjeldahl observed about similar works by Price, "[c]eramics express and are addressed to the hand. They acquire their full meaning within arm's reach, in the confiding zone — the ambit of embraces — where the sovereignty of sight blurs into that of touch."[57] And radiance? The beguiling and "glittering form" of *Ornette* is integrated with Price's masterfully subtle color, executed in a modulate range of variegated ruddy hues.[58]

But Neo-Thomist aesthetics won't stop there. With its breadth of philosophical wisdom from Aristotle to the present, this system of thought takes our apprehension of the beautiful to its transcendent source. The intelligibility of the beautiful is derived in the last analysis from the first intelligibility of the divine Ideas.[59] Schjeldahl may have his own sense of this in the "mindful joy" that he finds in Price's ceramic sculpture. "Isn't it a youthful inkling of such transcendence that gets somebody interested in art in the first place?"[60]

57. Schjeldahl, "Feats of Clay," p. 135.

58. Schjeldahl, "Feats of Clay," p. 133. Schjeldahl described Price's "fuchsia" as "metaphysical." See Maritain, "Art and Beauty," p. 163, n. 55: "the splendor or radiance of the form glittering on the beautiful object . . ."

59. Maritain, "Art and Beauty," pp. 163-64, n. 55.

60. Schjeldahl, "Feats of Clay," p. 135. In a post-post-analytical moment, I wondered if *Ornette* refers to the genius of the late Ornette Coleman, jazz saxophonist and trumpeter. Price's sculpture even has the look of an inverted trumpet oozing sensuous, viscous tones. A 1993 re-release of Coleman's work for Atlantic Records was titled, coincidentally, *Beauty Is a Rare Thing.*

A BROKEN BEAUTY AND ITS ARTISTS
Gordon Fuglie

5

When you are a person without the heavens, you also have very little Earth.

RABBI ADIN STEINSALTZ[1]

In the preceding chapter I described the basic conditions for beauty in a work of art as outlined by two mid-twentieth-century scholars, Jacques Maritain and Meyer Schapiro. I concluded the discussion with an example of my own apprehension of beauty in an encounter with a ceramic sculpture by contemporary artist Ken Price. This experience privileged my sense of pleasure and initiated an intuitive connection of my intellect with the sculpture. In such circumstances one may sense the purposes of the artist, and the very best of these encounters are marked by transcendence.

Critical readers would be correct to note that my encounter was with a small, relatively uncomplicated abstract form, and therefore the apprehension of beauty in Price's *Ornette* was destined to be a fairly straightforward experience. Such readers might further say that it is one thing to locate a basic definition of beauty in an elemental work and quite another to apprehend it in works of complexity — especially figurative works, or, further, those that are informed by narrative with a dramatic, somber, or melancholic nature.

My purpose in this chapter is to direct the discussion of beauty toward the artists and art in *A Broken Beauty* that have an affinity for spiritual or religious concerns and that are also informed by events of our times and the world we live in. In these works the basic conditions of beauty described in the previ-

ous chapter coexist with connections to and forays within the broad Judeo-Christian tradition and within art history. These connections and probes are often attempts to engage biblical texts in the light of recent or historic events — global, national, communal, or personal.

It is daunting to recall that the past century was marked by two world wars, the rise and fall of totalitarian political systems, the collapse of colonial empires, and civil wars and genocides almost too numerous to recollect. At the turn of this century there arose a swell of concerns about the sustainability of human life in a world increasingly driven by a global economy. What would be the economic and cultural consequences of a worldwide capitalism dominated by the West? This question is inseparable from the recognition that our air, land, and water are suffering toxic pollution and despoliation.

Concurrently, the triumph of the Western secularist outlook resulted in the narrowing of humanity's field of vision to the materiality of the world. Metaphysically, the "loss of the heavens," warns Rabbi Adin Steinsaltz, simultaneously means the downgrading of our life on Earth.[2] Artists, joining the chorus of environmentalists, would add that we have also lost our sense of the world's beauty. Materialist economics have fueled a lust in powerful nations to secure their lion's share of goods (and cheaply) at the expense of the less powerful. As materialism increasingly defines human life, the resultant dwarfing of our spiritual nature has left us disconnected from our innermost beings and in denial of our grieving souls. We are disconnected from one another, from nature, and from the transcendent. For many, and especially for the artists in *A Broken Beauty*, the road to reconnection leads to a

---

1. Quoted in the *Los Angeles Times*, July 16, 1988. A scholar, teacher, scientist, author and translator, mystic, and social critic, Steinsaltz is arguably the leading Jewish scholar of our age. He was born in 1937 to a secular Jewish family. He is best known for his interpretation, commentaries, translation, and publication of the Babylonian Talmud, an ongoing project.

2. Quoted in the *Los Angeles Times*, July 16, 1988.

quest for an authentic spirituality, and by extension, for authenticity in art.

Principal among the tasks of spiritual connection is the quest for a compelling narrative, a story that points to a way of being in the world. The great sacred texts of history, the Mahabharata, the Buddhist sutras, the Hebrew Scriptures, the Christian Testament, and the Qur'an offer in their own ways the wisdom against which humankind can measure the *Zeitgeist*. My own quest for an authoritative narrative has led to the Judeo-Christian tradition, with attention to its presence and absence in modern history. As a result, as an art historian and curator I have been especially interested to find artists who have connected with or examined this tradition in their work.

In the past fifteen years, throughout North America, there has been a notable blossoming of figurative, narrative, and religious-themed art that is derived from the Bible, examines the broad Judeo-Christian legacy, and utilizes narratives from contemporary life that relate to Scripture. Some of this work has a full-blown sensibility of our age, while others look to the wellspring of historical religious art while yet remaining firmly rooted in the concerns of the present.

One seasoned practitioner of this phenomenon is the Massachusetts painter Bruce Herman. Raised in the 1960s in an Episcopal environment that failed to slake his spiritual thirst, Herman was a quester early on. In high school he pored over sacred Hindu texts and became a disciple of Meher Baba, an Indian guru with disciples in North America. Moving up in the Baba sect, Herman became president of the Meher Baba Information Center in Cambridge in 1980. Two years later, disillusioned with what he saw as serious contradictions in his master's teaching, he renounced Baba and became a Christian — changing but continuing the quest.

During this time Herman was studying art, choosing figuration as his mode in the mid 1970s — a counterintuitive choice at a time when conceptual art and video were seen as the hot tickets to fame in The Art World (hereafter, TAW). Herman's inspiration for this direction was his encounter with the

triptychs of the German-American figurative artist Max Beckmann (1884-1950). As a graduate student at Boston University, Herman studied under figurative painters Philip Guston and James Weeks (see his Foreword). Following graduate school and his Christian conversion, Herman produced a series of realistic paintings, pastels, and monotypes with biblical subject matter and filled with the conviction of belief. In the late 1980s his work became more expressive and boldly limned; his current paintings tend to be large, to employ one or two figures, and to be composed of spiritually charged abstract planes.[3]

Herman is equally interested in the theology and history of Christianity and is an avid reader. With an outgoing temperament, Herman relishes the stimulation of artists who share his Christianity, or who draw on Judeo-Christian themes, or who reckon with the meaning of the body in contemporary art. Through a grant he received in 2001 he was able to host a gathering of such artists at rural Gordon College, where he teaches art and runs the campus gallery.[4] This later led to an exhibition and this book, taking up the current discussion of beauty within TAW, but adding to the mix the ancient Christian concept of human brokenness. Herman and many of his colleagues see a symbiotic relationship between beauty and brokenness that can shed light on our understanding of the human condition. The project's name, *A Broken Beauty,* is a notion borrowed from Simone Weil (1909-1943), a French philosopher of religious metaphysics.

3. Patricia Hanlon, *Golgotha: The Passion in Word and Image* (Wenham: Gordon College Publications, 1993); Patricia Hanlon, "Bruce Herman: A Profile," *IMAGE: A Journal of the Arts and Religion* 7 (Fall 1994): 31-44; David J. Goa, *The Body Broken: The Art of Bruce Herman,* exhibition catalog (Manchester: St. Anselm College/Alva deMars Megan Chapel Art Center, 2003).

4. The attendees at Herman's original gathering included Rick Harden (Connecticut), Jerome Witkin (Syracuse, NY), Tim Lowly and Joel Sheesley (Chicago), Edward Knippers (Washington, DC), Erica Grimm-Vance (Vancouver), and David J. Goa, an anthropologist and curator (Edmonton, Alberta). A year later additional artists were selected for inclusion in the project: Mary McCleary (Nacogdoches, TX), Gaela Erwin (Louisville, KY), Patty Wickman (Los Angeles), Melissa Weinman (Tacoma, WA), Gabrielle Bakker (Seattle), David Robinson (Vancouver), Stephen De Staebler (Berkeley, CA), and John Nava (Ojai, CA).

A Broken Beauty considers recent work of fifteen North American artists who deploy a variety of figurative and narrative modes. As Postmodern artists who matured in the twentieth century, they ponder the human condition and seek to push through superficial notions of human beauty and rethink figuration and narrative. This is evident when they introduce physical, mental, and spiritual brokenness into their depictions of human embodiment. The result is an upending of conventional idealizations of beauty. As viewers we are invited to consider the body's capacity for beauty *despite* its brokenness, *in the midst of* its brokenness, and, ironically, *because of* its brokenness. As Canadian anthropologist David J. Goa observes, "these works challenge us to be present to the struggle and grace emerging from deeply personal stories, historical and sacred narratives, and the terrors of history," those horrific events that overshadow and seep into our present and threaten to shape our future.

Thus artists in *A Broken Beauty* also join the discourse about beauty that broke out in the 1990s and is still seeking resolution. The various notions of beauty encountered in the works here, however, do not betray a yearning for some idealized "golden age," utopia, or a return to academic standards of beauty that marked official European and American art at the turn of the twentieth century. Rather, they seek a vision grounded in the realities of our present. And given the widespread global, national, and ethnic violence that marked the last hundred years, it will come as no surprise to twenty-first-century viewers that the humanity that the *Broken Beauty* artists draw, paint, and sculpt is marked by the long, sad legacy of that epoch — how could it not be and remain honest? But that legacy does not have the final word; the humanity and transcendence in their works also embody hope.

The discussion of the artists and art in *A Broken Beauty* is divided into six themes for this book and the related exhibition: After the Fall; Presence Encountered; The Terrors of History; The Mystery of Being; Sanctified; and Ecce Homo. My discussion will proceed in that thematic order.

After the Fall

Among the works produced by the artists in *A Broken Beauty,* I was surprised to find a number of images that dealt with chapters two, three, and four of the book of Genesis, the account of humankind's Edenic Fall and its consequences. Contemporary artists seeking TAW's blessing know that this is a subject deemed beyond the pale, though certain exemptions are granted to the "irrational savage," like black and Latino artists or the blue-collar lay preacher-cum artist, Howard Finster. These artists are usually found in the "folk art" or "outsider" genres, virtual Bantustans within TAW's empire. In these genres TAW permits religious themes to be charming entertainment, with quaint tableaux of a pre- or non-Fall Adam and Eve posed in a lush jungle, apple in hand, complete with a cute serpent appearing in a cameo role.

In addition to TAW's aversion to biblical imagery that is treated seriously by artists, it is also the case that the Bible itself has become a problematic text in North American culture. It is caught between resurgent fundamentalists, on the one hand, who see the Bible as an *object* to consult for one's salvation or an uncomplicated *source* of truth and knowledge, and militant skeptics on the other, who scornfully dismiss it because they believe its origins in the ancient world make the Bible an unevolved, barbarous text. Further, personal or group reading of the Bible has become burdened with "study," the search for *understanding,* instead of the potentially dislocating encounter with a transcendent reality that all sacred texts, and especially the Bible, desire to convey. Moreover, professional theologians have encumbered biblical narrative and poetry with form critical methodologies or probes beneath or behind Scripture to learn of the historical background informing the text.

Gabriel Josipovici, a literary critic, novelist, and playwright, is exasperated with these dampers on Bible reading and shows us a way out. "As readers we are not asked to understand, to extract meaning. Understanding is never at issue. We are asked to take

Figure 1. Gabrielle Bakker, *Eve and Her Conscience* (1998)

part."[5] Learned in the major texts of antiquity, Josipovici reminds us that, "Both Homer and the Bible, then, ask to be read aloud, even if only with the voice of the imagination. They ask not for an act of concentration or focusing but for what we might call relaxed participation. Surely, when we have read best in our lives we have read like that. We have read not to understand but to participate. No great book can ever come fully into focus. For focus suggests control and great books ask us to let go, to speak them, not to know them."[6] Speaking and participating, being available to what is said or seen in the moment of the encounter — something like this still happens in religious communities where spirited biblical proclamation is crucial in remembering the community's participation in God's covenant.

In a similar way, the participation of the seer is crucial to understanding Gabrielle Bakker's paintings of Eden and the tempted Eve.[7] Bakker's *Eve and Her Conscience,* done in a fourteenth- to fifteenth-century Italian Renaissance style, is one of a series she has produced on this theme (fig. 1). A diptych, its two pyramid-shaped figures are composed in separate panels. They are complemented and subtly linked by a smaller, inverted pyramid form that is made up of the mountains and the distant landscape overlapping the two panels in the lower half of the picture. This smaller pyramid is also the device connecting Eve and her personified, androgynous Conscience (he is not in the Genesis account), as is the brooding horizontal cloud that runs across the top of both panels, symbolizing her darkening state of mind.

Bakker's Eves are gendered, mythic protagonists struggling unsuccessfully with sin's seduction. In *Eve and Her Conscience,* the bust-length image of the two figures intimates our presence in the pictorial space. We become a participant in the appeal of Eve's conscience at the crucial moment when Eve has caved in to the serpent's deception and raises the forbidden fruit to her mouth. She avoids the earnest gaze of her conscience, who pleads with Eve for repentance, gesturing from his heart. As viewers we wonder: is Eve looking to and at *us* to be complicit in her sin, or are we meant to tip the balance in favor of the conscience, joining in his warning, turning her eyes back to his counsel? *Eve and Her Conscience* incorporates what biblical literary critic Robert Alter calls Eve and Adam's endowment with "a degree of morally problematic interiority," that is, their creation by God with the capacity to choose, or refuse, a relationship with the divine.[8] Bakker's Eve, severing her harmonious unity with her conscience, fractures the integrity of her being.

Edward Knippers's monumental, Baroque-flavored *The Harvest* depicts another moment of temptation (fig. 2).[9] In a binary composition, both Eve and Adam appear, seated beneath the Tree of the Knowledge of Good and Evil; one faces toward the viewer, the other faces away, creating a kind of revolving tension.

Knippers seems to imply that their eventful gathering beneath God's forbidden tree *must* lead to the eating of the fruit — it weighs in Eve's hand like an Olympic shot put. The image also foretells the darkening of their life by sin, as their complexions become ashen-dappled beneath the shade of the forbidden tree in the midst of God's radiantly verdant garden. Indeed, the shadow of the serpent creates a "mark" across Adam's back, the imprint of an irreversible transgression against God.

Genesis tells of the human condition before the Fall, male and female created by God, each necessary to the other for completeness and communion (see Genesis

---

5. Gabriel Josipovici, *Text and Voice: Essays, 1981-1991* (Manchester: Carcanet Press Limited, 1992), p. 30.

6. Josipovici, *Text and Voice,* pp. 30-31. See also his *The Book of God: A Response to the Bible* (New Haven: Yale University Press, 1988). I am also taken with Josipovici's notion of "relaxed participation" and its similarity to Maritain's description of the prepared intellect as it encounters and apprehends beauty. Notable, too, is Josipovici's assertion that "no great book can ever come into focus." This resembles Schapiro's claim that the conditions of beauty in a great work of visual art cannot be apprehended in one encounter (see my previous chapter). One can spend a lifetime reading Scripture as well as visiting the Sistine Chapel or Chartres and not exhaust their content.

7. Gabrielle Bakker interviewed by Debra Byrne, "A Conversation with the Artist," *Artifice and Representation: Paintings by Gabrielle Bakker,* exhibition catalog (Seattle: Frye Art Museum, 2002).

8. Robert Alter, *The Art of Biblical Literature* (New York: Basic Books, 1981), p. 29.

9. "A Primitive of an Old Way: An Interview with Edward Knippers," *Rutherford* 5, no. 12 (1996): 22-27; Theodore Prescott, "Edward Knippers," *IMAGE: A Journal of the Arts and Religion* 3 (Spring 1993).

Figure 2. Edward Knippers, *The Harvest (Adam and Eve)* (2002)

Figure 3. Joel Sheesley, *Nakedness on the Journey* (1997)

Figure 4. Joel Sheesley, *After Paradise* (2002)

1:27-28; 2:18, 21-25). In *The Harvest,* however, their sin makes for mutual sundering, embodied by Eve's sad blank gaze and their turning away from one another in numb contemplation of a beautiful paradise, now lost.

Joel Sheesley's *Nakedness on the Journey* moves the Genesis narrative to the expulsion from Eden (fig. 3). Here, portrayed as a white middle-class nightmare, a very naked forty-something Adam and Eve wander in the chilly autumnal wasteland, a ruin behind them. They aren't in suburbia anymore.

Sheesley's rendering of the couple's flesh is not unlike the work of New York painter Philip Pearlstein, discussed by Theodore Prescott in an earlier chapter. There is, however, an important difference between the two. Pearlstein portrays the human body with an eye simply to the forms of flesh as it is affixed to bone and from a perspective devoid of narrative or literary references. Sheesley also paints flesh in a nonidealized manner, but this approach lends a sense of pathos, vulnerability, to his figures. And while his settings are not dramatic, they do resonate with subtle narrative associations. We desire to learn the story underlying the plight of this contemporary Adam and Eve.

Like Bakker's Eve, Sheesley's figures gaze at the viewer as if to bring us into their situation. The couple's grim, shocked expressions mirror our beholding of them. Framed and fenced in by a tangled dark wood, they — and we — are on a bleak journey after the Fall.

After Paradise is another post-Fall image by Sheesley. At first, disregarding its alerting title, it seems to be a rather dumb photorealist picture of a middle-class suburban bedroom, until we take in the details (fig. 4). The artist believes that the natural and human realms are fruitful for his paintings: "because of the precedent of [Christ's] Incarnation, people and objects in the visible world can be imbued with symbolic meaning."[10] And so they are here. The split

"his/hers" closet, a post-Fall device in a contemporary setting, delineates the alienation of the male and female from each other, their separate behaviors and realms enclosed in darkness. And though two figures were originally intended for inclusion in the composition, their absence more effectively suggests their presence. Further, the framed print on the wall merits our scrutiny. It is an engraving by the Flemish Renaissance artist Jan Gossaert (c. 1478-1532), also called Mabuse, and was a thinly veiled excuse for making a pornographic image. Pruriently, it suggests that Adam and Eve's sexual lust initiated their lust for the knowledge of good and evil. No such notion exists in Genesis, though it was certainly active in Gossaert's post-Fall imagination! Thus another layer of narrative gets added to our encounter with Sheesley's painting. We see the alienation of the man and woman in the ancient Genesis story played out in a contemporary suburban bedroom, commented on by a sixteenth-century artist whose image looks down on the nuptial bed, all filtered through the viewer's awareness of Freudian psychology.

Mary McCleary's obsessively crafted collage on paper, *Children of the Apple Tree,* takes place in the generations succeeding Adam and Eve (fig. 5).[11] Their offspring, also the descendents of Cain, are now locked into cycles of violence. In viewing the children's surroundings — another garden — there is an attempt to deny the violence inherent in our human condition: the "new gardeners" have done their best to shape and trim the post-Fall garden into an ordered pastoral, a pleasant park, reviving that nostrum of social engineering: beautify the environment and you beautify human nature. McCleary's work is composed entirely of shards and fragments — the throwaways from popular consumer culture,

10. Author's interview with the artist, July 23, 2002. See also John Walford, "Joel C. Sheesley," *IMAGE: A Journal of the Arts and Religion* 4 (Fall 1993): 23-36; Wayne Roosa, "Signs of Consciousness, Pilgrimage and Presence in the Paintings of Joel Sheesley," *Sheesley/Witkin: Fortitude and Forbearance,* exhibition catalog (Grand Rapids: Center Art Gallery, Calvin College, 2001), pp. 6-19; Ed Krantz, *The Painted Journey: Works by Joel Sheesley,* exhibition catalog (Elgin: Safety-Kleen Gallery One, Elgin Community College, 2002).

11. Wayne L. Roosa, "A Fullness of Vision: Mary McCleary's Collages," *IMAGE: A Journal of the Arts and Religion* 23 (1999): 32-42; Dana Friis-Hansen and Gregory Wolfe, *Mary McCleary, Beginning with the Word, Constructed Narratives: 1985-2000,* exhibition catalog (Galveston: Galveston Art Center, 2000); interview with the artist by James Romaine, "Conversation with Mary McCleary," *Objects of Grace: Conversations on Creativity and Faith* (Baltimore: Square Halo Books, 2002), pp. 51-62.

reconfigured to make beauty and a narrative out of brokenness. A close scrutiny of the garden, however, will lead the searching viewer to a hopeful clue. Scavenged by the artist and mounted on the tree at the right is a small ornamental brass Christmas tree with children dancing around it. It is a signifier of joy at the birth of the Prince of Peace, the "New Adam," whose incarnational work enables humankind to reverse the perennial violence and scapegoating acted out in the garden below.[12]

Presence Encountered

Throughout the twentieth century, few Modernist artists chose the Virgin Mary, the Mother of Jesus, as a subject of their art, unless they happened to receive a rare commission from an ecclesiastical institution. As a subject with a long train of pre-Modern baggage and some peculiar doctrines in the nineteenth and twentieth centuries, she became even more of an anachronism in secular society and Modernist cultural circles than her illustrious Son.[13] Meanwhile, within popular Catholicism in the Americas, interest in and devotion to her continued unabated.[14]

    With the spread of Postmodernism in the 1970s,

however, the consideration of previously ignored art and artists widened. This coincided with the emergence of Chicano and Latino art on the West coast and in the American Southwest in the 1980s.[15] Many in the first wave of these artists had roots in the Mexican-American civil rights movement and utilized traditional and popular Catholic imagery in their work, often with socio-political overtones. Sympathetic galleries blossomed to show this work, whose subject often included the Virgin Mary, and especially the Virgin of Guadalupe, the latter a source of spiritual solace, Latino religious identity within Anglo society, and female strength in the Mexican-American community. The combination of social justice and ethnic identity amounted to a cultural preemptive strike against any resistance that TAW might have to earnest Marian content. Thus she was "permitted" as a subject for Chicano artists because she was an expression of *their* culture, but this also meant that she — along with most other Mexican-American art — could be isolated within a TAW Bantustan of "Latino" or "Chicano Art," separate from TAW's notion of contemporary art. Even though a taboo on religious subject matter had been broken and a precedent established, Mary would remain an unwelcome subject in contemporary art for most non-Latino artists.[16]

    This, however, has not discouraged curious artists from engaging Marian subjects. Bruce Herman's monumental *Annunciation* from his *Elegy for Witness*

---

12. Mary McCleary, along with a number of the artists in *A Broken Beauty,* has become interested in the theories of René Girard (b. 1923), who, using anthropological methods in his reading of Judeo-Christian texts as well as secular literature, devised a theory of mimetic rivalry, human conflict, and the scapegoat to understand historical and contemporary social violence. Girard, who converted to Catholicism in middle age, believes that the Bible's distinct sympathy for the victim, ultimately and redemptively embodied in Jesus' life and sacrifice, points to a way out of endless cycles of violence of all kinds. See James G. Williams, ed., *The Girard Reader* (New York: Crossroad, 1996).

13. Non-Catholic readers may be surprised to learn that in 1854 — three years after the Great Exhibition in London, in which the capitalist world's manufactured goods were displayed in the steel and glass Crystal Palace — a new status was conferred on Mary, the new doctrine of her Immaculate Conception, that is, her birth without the stain of original sin. A century later, in the Atomic Age, Pope Pius XII defined the Assumption of her body and soul into heaven at her death. Neither doctrine can be justified biblically.

14. For a positive, judicious assessment, see Jaroslav Pelikan, *Mary Through the Centuries: Her Place in the History of Culture* (New Haven: Yale University Press, 1998); for a more skeptical view, see Marina Warner, *Alone of All of Her Sex: The Myth and Cult of the Virgin Mary,* rev. ed. (London: Random House, 2000).

15. Richard Griswold Castillo et al., *Chicano Art: Resistance and Affirmation, 1965-1985* (Los Angeles: Wight Art Gallery, UCLA, 1991), covers the formative years. In addition, Chicano art has not received sufficient credit for its role in "reintroducing" the human figure and narrative into contemporary painting in the 1970s and 1980s.

16. J. Michael Walker, an Anglo artist from Los Angeles who draws in a style reminiscent of Mexican colonial painting, has had difficulty placing his work in local commercial galleries because of his ethnicity, despite the fact that he married into a Mexican family and is fluent in Spanish. TAW was willing to go to the mat, however, in defense of aberrant depictions of the Virgin such as Afro-British artist Chris Ofili's controversial image of her emblazoned with elephant dung and surrounded by collaged pornographic images. Readers will recall the scandal Ofili's painting caused in the Brooklyn Museum of Art's showing of *Sensations* in 1999, when then New York Mayor Rudolph Giuliani attempted to get the work removed from the exhibition and cut off the museum's funding. Predictably, TAW responded by rallying around its sacred oriflamme, the first amendment, to protect Ofili's inclusion in *Sensations.*

series shows us that non-Latino artists can claim her, too (fig. 6). He has limned her in a fashion that braids abstraction with figuration. Mary's body on the right becomes suffused with the sacred, whose domain occupies the left-hand panel in dynamic planes of white, sky blue, silver, and gold. Surprisingly, Mary's nudity here presents no scandal to the viewer, in part because the artist uses Classical form to convey her vulnerability.

Historically, the Classical figure has been the human ideal of beauty in Western art. But Herman's use of Classicism subverts the ideal. To convey Mary's self-acknowledged humility and humanity in response to the angel Gabriel's annunciation of the divine Word ("You see before you the Lord's servant, let it happen to me as you have said," Luke 1:38),[17] her body has been formed with applications of pigment that are then abraded, added to, abraded again, and so on — the Classical body as ruin. As a result her beauty is built on a series of ruptures; indeed, her arms are fractured or missing — a Christian Venus de Milo. Herman implies that our brokenness is the condition in which we are most receptive to God and in which a redemptive beauty can emerge. In his iconography, Mary's humility in obedience to divine purpose is portrayed as a physical fracturing.

Female adolescence in the American suburbs is where Patty Wickman sets her Annunciation in her large pastel-toned canvas, *Overshadowed* (fig. 7). The work has parallels to the suburban narratives of Eric Fischl, though in contrast to Fischl's ambiguity, clues to the Marian content of *Overshadowed* are accessible through a close reading of the scene.

In the solitude of her disarrayed bedroom, a teenage girl kneels in wary fascination before the white glow of a bare-bulb lamp. By crossing her arms in front of her chest, she "causes" a winged shape to be shadowed upon her chemise at abdomen level. A telephone handset strewn on the floor is a signifier of the angelic messenger from heaven, the vehicle

for the voice/Word of God. In Catholic theology the "overshadowing" of the Virgin by the procreative Word commences "the mysteries of the Mystical Body [the Church], . . . [first] generated in the womb of the virginal Church."[18]

Melissa Weinman's large pseudo-altarpiece was inspired by Jan Polack's *Schutzmantelmadonna* from 1510 in Munich's *Frauenkirche,* which she discovered while on an artist's fellowship in Germany.[19] The *Schutzmantelmadonna* is a traditional Marian image that shows her as an archetypal protectress, a function visualized by her great cape that envelops the faithful who are portrayed in the foreground. It was a type especially popular in Northern Europe during the late Middle Ages up to the Protestant Reformation. Polack's Mary impressed Weinman with her vitality and energy, her bodying forth suggesting a joyous — even erotic — dance to the artist, who resolved to do a contemporary version of it.

The contemporary model for Weinman's Mary is a young Mexican-German woman who is also a dancer and who the artist felt conveyed the vitality of Polack's Virgin (fig. 8). Among the devoted faithful in the foreground are Weinman's friends, with the artist in her painter's smock at the far left. Using a symmetrical and triangular composition, unified by Mary's central placement, the artist has drawn on Marian theology to portray the Virgin's great mantle as an extension of her body. The red interior suggests her sheltering womb, the white exterior her skin and purity.[20] In the background, looming behind the mantle of the radiantly beauti-

17. All Scripture cited in this essay is from *The New Jerusalem Bible* (New York: Doubleday, 1985).

18. Since the Middle Ages, the body of Mary has been equated with the church as an enclosing *corpus* for God's people, the community redeemed by her Son, Jesus, who was sheltered in her womb and is the Head of the Church. On Marian theology, see Hans Urs von Balthasar, *The Glory of the Lord: A Theological Aesthetics,* volume 1: *Seeing the Form,* trans. Erasmo Leiva-Merikakis (San Francisco: Ignatius Press, 1982), pp. 338-43.

19. Ruth Weisberg, *Melissa Weinman: Saint's Stories, Viewpoints,* exhibitions catalog (Seattle: Frye Art Museum, 1997).

20. Balthasar, *The Glory of the Lord,* p. 340, is instructive: "Mary, by bearing and giving birth to her Son, the Head of the Church, encloses all Christians within herself and brings them forth from herself along with their experience of faith, and this is a relationship with them which is somehow *physical.* The archetype, by its very nature, has a maternal form and under its 'protective mantle' it embraces the progeny that will imitate it" (emphasis added).

Figure 5. Mary McCleary, *Children of the Apple Tree* (2000)

Figure 6. Bruce Herman, *Annunciation,* from the series *Elegy for Witness* (2002)

Figure 7. Patty Wickman, *Overshadowed* (2001)

ful Virgin, are the horrors that endanger the fragile human band that gathers in the foreground: scarred battlefields, bombed and ruined cities, and mass graves — a world broken and disfigured by twentieth-century warfare.

The Terrors of History

For Melissa Weinman, a contemporary depiction of the Virgin sheltering humanity with her protective mantle meant taking into account the horrific global violence that was a backdrop of life in the twentieth century. In the paintings of Jerome Witkin and Richard Harden, this violence — the Holocaust, cycles of ethnic cleansing and warfare — is brought into the foreground as the main subject.

No contemporary American artist has so relentlessly and fearlessly sought to come to grips with the meaning of the Holocaust, the *Shoah,* as New York painter Jerome Witkin.[21] Half Jewish on his father's side, he has for the past twenty years immersed himself in the horror of the Nazi "Final Solution," producing large serial narrative canvases that have caused many viewers to turn aside in empathic grief.

Entering Darkness from 2002 comprises six irregularly shaped consecutive panels and completes his engagement with the Holocaust (fig. 9). To correspond with Hebrew script, Witkin has arranged the panels to read from right to left. The series was inspired by his reading of a diary entry from an evangelical Christian nurse from Minnesota, Dorothy Wahlstrom, who was among the first to enter the Dachau concentration camp after its Allied liberation in 1945.[22] Witkin decided that Wahlstrom should be the protagonist in his narrative, and she

appears in every panel but one. Bearing a flashlight as she traverses the murky barracks, she is also the surrogate for the viewer's journey, serving as our Virgil, the guide who escorted the poet Dante Alighieri through Hell's inferno in *The Divine Comedy.* Like Wahlstrom the nurse — the one who tends and ministers to the suffering — we must make the journey through the camp to ultimately discover the demonic political ideology that harnessed lethal industrial methods and a perverted medical technology to break the minds, spirits, and bodies of the prisoners of Dachau.

Witkin insists that our journey can be completed only if we come face to face with evil's source; otherwise we will lack the moral resolve to stop future holocausts. Panel five is the focus of this encounter and the most harrowing and dramatic, as well as the largest of the series. Wahlstrom, flashlight in hand, stands on a rickety, partially destroyed bridge. Amid the ruins and the conflagration of European civilization, a monstrous Hitler demon, the personification of evil, rises and lunges at her. But the nurse's resolve is unshakable, and guided by her light, she makes her way through and past the raging, shattered surroundings. In panel six, in the quiet of the barracks, her journey done, Wahlstrom can now rest, though she is changed forever. In the background, a free prisoner — now healthy and restored to himself — strides out of the camp to a new day and a hopeful life.

After Connecticut artist Richard Harden journeyed to the Balkans in the immediate wake of the region's civil wars and ethnic cleansing in the 1990s, he was moved to abandon a successful career in printmaking to become a painter of twentieth-century history on the scale, if not the style, of Anselm Kiefer. Unlike his German counterpart, Harden's huge paintings deploy a rich repertoire of accessible imagery, and thus are a more direct symbolic and metaphorical response to the violent history of the region. Hugely popular in the Balkans, his paintings have been shown in Belgrade, Pristina, Kosova, Sarajevo, and Skopje, where Harden says they have "helped catalyze multi-ethnic audiences in important self-reflection and discussion of questions often bur-

21. Albert Boime discusses *Entering Darkness* in "Which Came First: The Cosmos or the Chaos?" *Cosmos & Chaos: A Cultural Paradox,* exhibition catalog (Binghampton: Roberson Museum & Science Center, 2004), pp. 16-19. For a general biographical treatment of Witkin, see Sherry Chayat, *Life Lessons: The Art of Jerome Witkin* (Syracuse: Syracuse University Press, 1994). At this writing an updated revision is in the works. See also Joel C. Sheesley, "Jerome Witkin: A Profile," *IMAGE: A Journal of the Arts and Religion* 11 (Fall 1995): 22-32.

22. Rhoda G. Lewin, ed., *Witnesses to the Holocaust: An Oral History* (New York: Twayne Publishers, 1989).

Figure 8. Melissa Weinman, *Schutzmantelmadonna* (1996-1997)

ied by persistent national mythology, taut political posturing and identity politics."[23]

Like the shifting currents of Balkan history, Harden's panels can be repositioned for each installation, inviting multiple narrative understandings. The configuration selected for *A Broken Beauty* creates the panoramic triptych *My Breath* (fig. 10). At the center, the viewer rests his eyes on an impressionistic poppy field near Sarajevo in late spring, then recoils at the discovery of human skeletal remains among the feathery grass and bright flowers. With this mordantly ironic painting, Harden becomes, in effect, the anti–Claude Monet; there are no soothing, sun-dappled, aqueous surfaces dotted by lily pads here. He adds to the irony by placing two panels of single female nudes, both titled *Falling,* as the triptych's bookends. One hundred years ago, the female nude was the unquestioned ideal of natural and human beauty (see fig. 1 in the previous chapter). Here their bodies whirl helplessly, perilously, in free-fall within a vortex of cinder and ash — their idealism unsustainable in a season of arson, gang rape, and murder.

The Mystery of Being

Our bodily existence is intertwined with our interiority, that is, our capacity to reflect upon life and choose among a range of possibilities for action. A number of works in *A Broken Beauty* image the question of what it means to be an enfleshed, reasoning being, even expanding our limits on who counts as "fully" human. We also need to acknowledge our animal appetites. Yet, even as we satisfy these appetites, we find ourselves filled with spiritual longing, desiring transcendence. We need food, yes; and we need meaning.

Such a range of human concerns has long been embodied in the figurative sculpture of Northern Californian artist Stephen De Staebler, whose

marred-yet-elegant figures simultaneously root themselves in their base, the earth, while stretching into the sky.[24] *Yoke-Winged Man* (fig. 11), an attenuated bronze form, whose heart is ablaze in red, simultaneously suggests the crucified Christ, a blessing angel, and a mortal in existential struggle with twin destinies: the world wherein we live and die; and the heavenly realm, our truest home, which we hope for with our innermost being.

The incompleteness, the missing limbs, and the scarring of the human form, as well as the agglomeration of rude, geological masses onto De Staebler's figures, are all devices that underscore our creaturely imperfection and finitude. Eschewing ideal form, they evoke our sense of compassion for the reality of our existence.

The artist's dogged insistence on the figure, his frequent use of religious themes, and his desire to draw on and continue the humanistic sculptural tradition during the reign of Abstract Expressionism and other later trends into the 1990s placed De Staebler just under TAW's radar. With the discussion of beauty and the body now under way, however, it is hoped that De Staebler will receive the national recognition he deserves.[25]

Erica Grimm-Vance of Vancouver credits De Staebler as a major influence, and she seeks similar ends in her painting.[26] Working in the seemingly opposing forms of raw industrial steel sheets and the ancient medium of encaustic (wax blended with pigment) painting, her images are drawn from models who are professional dancers and yoga practitioners, virtuosos of physical beauty and body mastery. From their poses, Grimm-Vance depicts beings that are

23. A number of these paintings have also been acquired by regional Balkan museums. See Richard Harden, *In a Field of Poppies: An Installation Creating Dialogue for Peace and Understanding,* self-published exhibition catalog, unpaginated (Pleasant Valley, CT, 2002).

24. Doug Adams, "Becoming One Body: Stephen De Staebler's Family of Winged Figures," *IMAGE: A Journal of the Arts and Religion* 37 (Winter 2002/3): 29-36; Ramsay Ball Breslin, "The Figure as Fragment: The Sculpture of Stephen De Staebler," *Stephen De Staebler: Recent Work,* exhibition catalog (San Francisco: Thiebaud Gallery, 1994); Donald Kuspit, *Stephen De Staebler: The Figure,* exhibition catalog (San Francisco: Chronicle Books, 1988).

25. De Staebler's last retrospective was in 1988; it traveled only in the Western United States to regional museums.

26. Tim Bascom, "A Beautiful Affliction: The Art of Erica Grimm-Vance," *IMAGE: A Journal of the Arts and Religion* 31 (Summer 2001): 26-35.

shown straining upward with exertion — and pain — toward the divine, in works such as *Swimming in Existence: The Cloud of Unknowing* and *With Great Effort We Remembered* (figs. 12 and 13).

The dark empty expanses of her sheets of steel are reclaimed by the artist as "planes of silence," evoking the *apophatic* (voiceless) state of prayer of the Christian East. She says her imagery is prompted by her reflection on French philosopher Simone Weil's observation of a paradox of human experience: within the body there is a coexistence of beauty and affliction, and mysteriously therein is found the image of God and the desire of the divine to communicate with our souls. Such insights are currently unwelcome in TAW, but Grimm-Vance remains undaunted: "I know that beauty and spirituality are both taboo. Thus the only way to get to either is via a raw beauty. If you portray beauty in a raw way, then you can get to some truth."[27]

Her fellow Canadian, sculptor David Robinson, is after a divine discovery, too, though with an entirely different sensibility.[28] With meticulous craft and skill — and a dose of wry humor — Robinson plays with the notion of the global businessman who seeks to conquer the realm of commerce and stand on top of the world. Once there, he discovers that he has somehow arrived on holy ground (also the title of the work, fig. 14), encountering a transcendence that commands his humility. Like the biblical Moses, and other traditions of the sacred, he removes his shoes.

Since 1988 Chicago painter Tim Lowly has cradled the head of his severely retarded daughter Temma and asked, What does it mean to be a human being without any apparent cognitive capacities or mobility?[29] *Carry Me* (fig. 15) is a composite view of his immobile daughter, who is offered up as an answer:

carry me, this is who I am, broken in mind, broken in body. But this encounter turns our questions on ourselves. How do I regard Temma? Do I see my own humanity in her ultra-marginalized physicality? Or am I on holy ground, standing with God, who regards Temma with his merciful gaze? In this monochromatic drawing-as-painting, Temma is held aloft — presented to us — by six young women (art students of Lowly's at North Park University) who fix us with their gentle, expectant gaze, awaiting our answer.

Sanctified

The Canadian anthropologist David Goa calls our attention to a long and alternate tradition of Christian thought that sees the "sanctified life," sainthood, not as some sort of purity or conventional norm of piety, but as what happens when people recover their capacity to be fully present to the world. In this understanding, true sanctity comes when our ideals and expectations fall away, and the resulting void and loss that we feel are filled with compassion toward what *is,* the real. The various saints (both obvious and less so) gathered in *A Broken Beauty* come to ecstasy or beauty, not through some romantic spiritual experience, but in the midst of what is given in the course of life.

In secular educated circles, saints are still something of a joke; they are seen as sentimental, irrational caricatures of outmoded norms of behavior. We moderns prefer leaner, up-to-date notions of virtue, such as an integrity shaped only by Enlightenment rationality to serve the needs of *this* world. Occasionally, however, someone from these circles will have pause to rethink their secularism. If during a vacation to India someone had visited Calcutta and by chance met the diminutive, radiant Mother Teresa, who ran a hospice for the city's legions of destitute and dying homeless, their secular conceptions about the world might well have been shaken.

In the realm of medieval scholarship, secular biases left saints and their cults largely unstudied through much of the twentieth century. In 1982 the

27. Bascom, "A Beautiful Affliction," p. 27.

28. *Levitas/Gravitas: The Sculpture of David Robinson,* essays by Sarah Dobbs and Bruce Van Slyke (Vancouver: Tracey Lawrence Gallery, 2002); see also: www.robinsonstudio.com.

29. Fred Camper, "Temma Lowly and the Meaning of Life," *Chicago Reader,* section 1, November 22, 2002; Karen Halvorsen-Schreck, *Trouble the Water: Paintings by Tim Lowly,* exhibition catalog (Santa Barbara: Westmont College/Reynolds Gallery, 2002). See also the artist's website: www.timlowly.com.

Figure 9. Jerome Witkin, *Entering Darkness* (2001), six panels, to be viewed from right to left

Figure 10. Richard Harden, *My Breath,* flanked by two panels, both entitled *Falling* (2001)

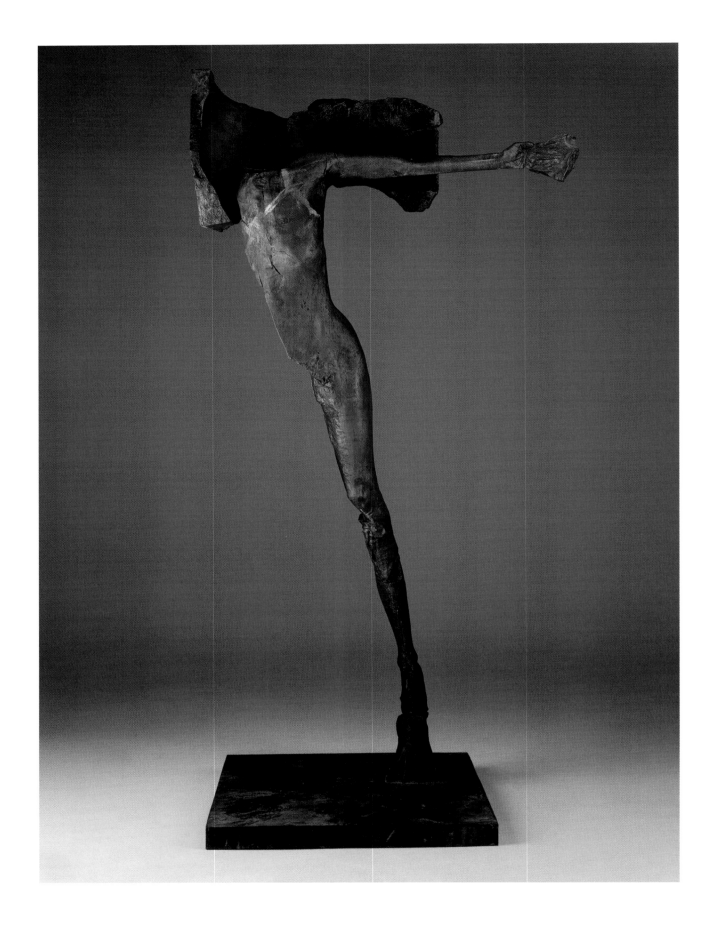

Figure 11. Stephen De Staebler, *Yoke-Winged Man* **(1994)**

Figure 12. Erica Grimm-Vance, *Swimming in Existence: The Cloud of Unknowing* (1999-2001)

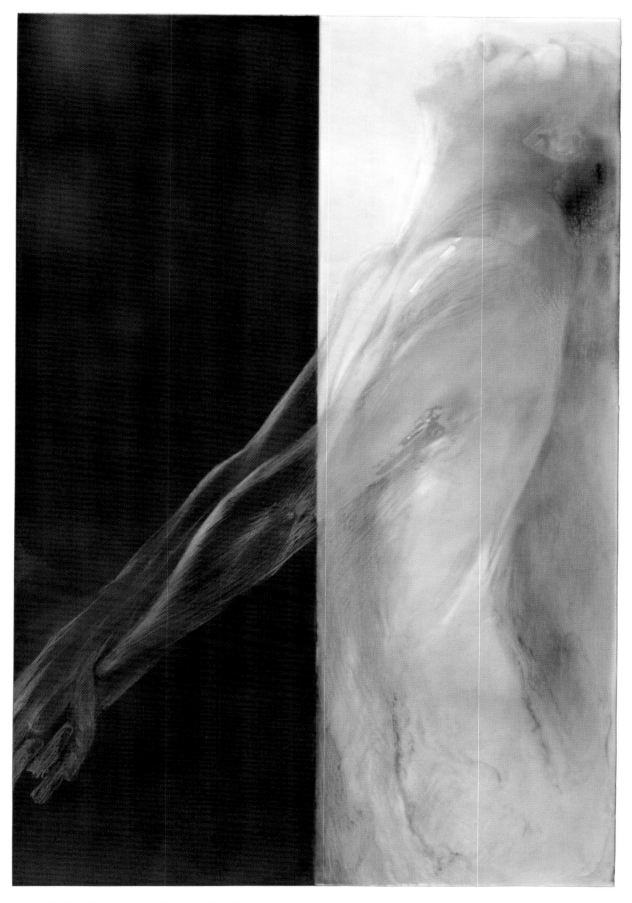

Figure 13. Erica Grimm-Vance, *With Great Effort We Remembered* (2002)

Figure 14. David Robinson, *On Holy Ground* (1999)

Figure 15a. Timothy Grubbs Lowly, *Carry Me* (2002)

Figure 15b. Timothy Grubbs Lowly, *Carry Me,* detail (2002)

deeply learned, urbane, and compassionate Peter Brown opened up the rich and complex world of sainthood in Late Antiquity with his *The Cult of the Saints*. This work propelled research about religion in the Middle Ages in a number of new directions.[30]

In the section on the theme "Presence Encountered," I discussed the importance of Chicano and Mexican-American art for the resurgence of figuration, narrative, and intended religious content in the contemporary art world, especially with the subject of the Virgin Mary. In addition, many of these artists have developed new iconographies for the Virgin and the lives of the saints. On the West coast, Anglo artists J. Michael Walker and Patty Wickman in Los Angeles, and Melissa Weinman in Tacoma, were spurred by these examples and felt free to open up a once-taboo subject with a wider and more lively repertoire of imagery and narrative.

As her hagiography goes, Saint Agatha was an early Christian martyr from Sicily who suffered numerous cruel tortures because she spurned the amorous overtures of a pagan Roman senator. Among these tortures was the severing of her breasts, a mutilation that evokes strong empathy from female artists. Paintings by Patty Wickman and Melissa Weinman depict this aspect of Agatha's martyrdom from different standpoints, bringing the saint's plight into the present day.

Wickman's *Anonymous (with St. Agatha)* (fig. 16) works on two levels. Lovingly appropriating a Baroque altarpiece panel by Francisco Zurbaran, the painting within Wickman's painting pays homage to the pious legend of the saint, who, holding her severed breasts on a platter, gazes at the viewer with stoic calm. At left is a nude woman from the 1990s who advances into the viewer's space and raises a silicone gel breast implant in each hand for our consideration, a form of offering.[31] These alien, synthetic objects will be inserted and sewn into her

body, a surgery that involves slicing an arc beneath the breast or making a circumference cut to remove the nipple and aureole. This is a perverted, superficial quest for physical beauty and perfection. The digital patterning Wickman overlays on the genitals, breasts, and face of the woman imply a loss of identity and personhood. By contrast, the Agatha legend extols a woman attaining bodily and spiritual perfection by reserving herself as a vessel for God.

In her treatment of the saint, Weinman evokes the feeling of Agatha's mutilation and her loss in *St. Agatha's Grief,* using an unmistakably contemporary young model (fig. 17). Shrouded in darkness, a "before" image of Agatha awaits her fate at the hand of her torturers. The "after" Agatha raises her face to mourn her loss to God and is bathed in healing light. Like Wickman's double image of the saint, Weinman says that the painting also works as a memorial to friends who have suffered breast cancer and is in general a eulogy on male violence against women. *St. Agatha's Grief* achieves a delicate balance of horror and dignity in suffering.

Edith Stein was raised in a German Jewish family, became an agnostic as a teenager, studied phenomenological philosophy at university, and converted to Catholicism, taking holy orders as a Discalsed Carmelite nun in 1934, when the Nazis denied public writing and publishing to all Jews in Germany. As Teresa Benedicta of the Cross, she wrote extensively within the convent. She was eventually arrested by the Nazis and sent to Auschwitz, where she was murdered in 1942.[32] In a controversial act, Pope John Paul II canonized her in 1998.[33] Jerome Witkin, who was born of a Jewish father and an Italian Catholic mother, memorializes her final days in *Between a Ladder and Smoke,* a painting executed in somber monochromes and stark iconic two-dimensionality (fig. 18). With the Nazi-mandated yellow star of David on her habit and her hand on an hourglass,

30. Peter Brown, *The Cult of the Saints: Its Rise and Function in Latin Christianity* (London: SCM Press, 1981). See also his *Society and the Holy in Late Antiquity* (Berkeley: University of California, 1982), and numerous later works.

31. Gordon Fuglie, "Passion Paintings: The Art of Patty Wickman," *IMAGE: A Journal of the Arts and Religion* 25 (Winter 1999/2000): 27-33.

32. Waltrud Herbstrith, *Edith Stein: A Biography* (New York: Harper & Row, 1985).

33. John Sullivan, OCD, STD, ed., *Holiness Befits Your House: Canonization of Edith Stein: A Documentation* (Washington, DC: ICS Publications, 2000). Starting in 1986, ICS has begun issuing her complete works in English.

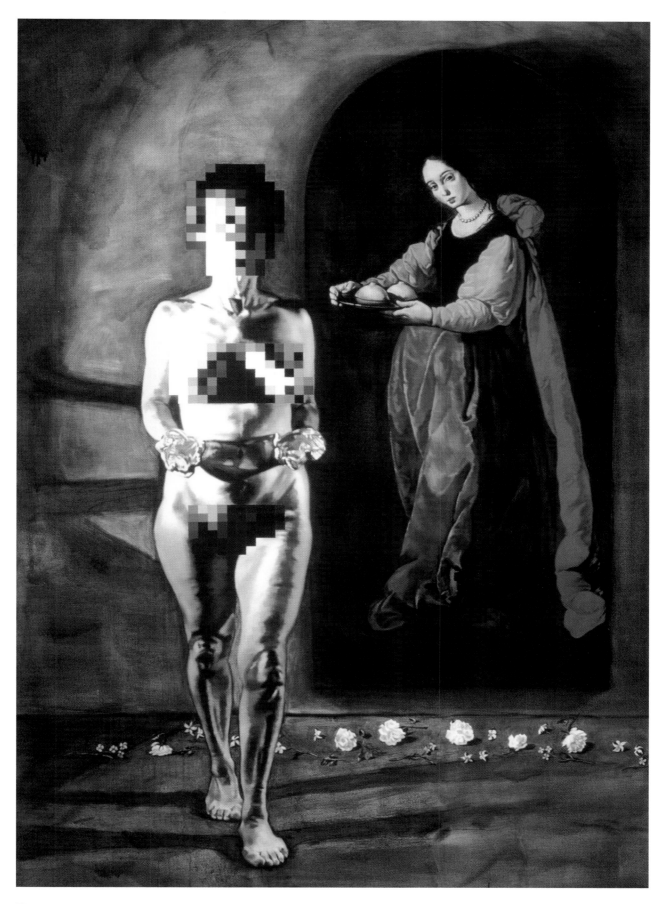

Figure 16. Patty Wickman, *Anonymous (with St. Agatha)* (1996)

Figure 17. Melissa Weinman, *St. Agatha's Grief* (1996)

Figure 18. Jerome Witkin, *Between a Ladder and Smoke: Edith Stein* (1997)

Stein, drawing on the spiritual reserves of her rich inner life, turns to God for sustenance and courage. The title suggests her martyrdom in the Auschwitz crematorium and her heavenly destination.

Another Christian victim of the Third Reich was the Evangelical Lutheran pastor, theologian, ecumenist, and member of the anti-Nazi resistance, Dietrich Bonhoeffer.[34] One of his more poignant meditations concerned how Jesus found it possible to live and work in the midst of his enemies, an inspiration for Bonhoeffer's political action. In *Bonhoeffer* (fig. 19), from his series *Elegy for Witness*, Bruce Herman paints the moment of the pastor's martyrdom, when he was hanged by the Gestapo in 1945. The backdrop of the upper part of the painting is patterned with architectural lattice work, the ruins of Germany; the bottom is covered in gold leaf, the realm of God. This may be the first painting in which a martyr descends into the divine. As his head and shoulders plunge into the golden realm, Bonhoeffer's life pours into it in radiant aureate streams.

In the 1990s, in the wake of another and later European war, Richard Harden traveled through the Balkans with his sketchbooks, drawing the faces of the young people he met. Back in the United States, he digitally scanned his drawings, photographs, and memorabilia from his journeys, producing large-format digital collages based on his portraits. *Nenad* (fig. 20), the name of a Serbian art student and the title of one of Harden's collages, reveals a young man in anxiety over the fate of his land and people. It is an icon of sorts, one handsome young Serb gazing into — and hoping for — a future free of ethnic warfare. From this and his other sketches, Harden concluded, "humans are both more beautiful and fractured than we can understand."[35]

Tim Lowly's twelve-inch-square painting entitled *In Ekstasis*, "in ecstasy" (fig. 21), is a portrait of his

severely retarded young daughter Temma. It, too, conveys an iconic sensibility. Technically, the work is based upon a photograph, a snapshot with minimal aesthetic presence. In this regard Lowly's work reminds us of the contemporary German painter Gerhard Richter, whose dependence on unartistic photographs has actually made his paintings more intriguing, more mysterious. Not to be mistaken for mere Photorealism, that deadpan yet precise rendering of the nondescript American social landscape of the 1970s, the in-and-out-of-focus Temma in *In Ekstasis* works its way into our consciousness. And this reverses our anxious impulse to make her a non-person, relegating her to the farthest reaches of Otherness — out of our sight and awareness. After all, we know that Temma cannot become a projection of our dreams and ideals or ever be the measure of conventional notions of beauty and desire. Yet, as the writer Karen Halvorsen-Schreck notes, this uncanny portrait icon becomes "an exploration of how her appearance makes manifest her interior life — or the allusive mystery of her interior life."[36] The portrait does not try to sum up its subject. Lowly's painting asks us to be present to what and who Temma is — mysteries both.

Ecce Homo

There is, as it were, an incarnation of God in the World, and it is indicated by beauty.[37]

Simone Weil

At the end of the twentieth century, a wide range of scholarly and cultural endeavors tried to reckon with Jesus Christ from new perspectives. In North America, the historians and theologians who made up the controversial Jesus Seminar renewed the effort to place Jesus in the historical context of his time.[38] Their research and the work of other scholars

34. Eberhard Bethge, *Dietrich Bonhoeffer: Theologian, Christian, Man for His Times,* rev. and ed. Victoria J. Barnett, trans. Eric Mosbacher (Minneapolis: Fortress Press, 2000). See John W. de Gruchy, *The Cambridge Companion to Dietrich Bonhoeffer* (New York: Cambridge University Press, 1999), for a bibliography of Bonhoeffer's writings in English translation.

35. Interview with the artist, June 2, 2002.

36. Halvorsen-Schreck, *Trouble the Water,* p. 4.

37. George Panichas, ed., *The Simone Weil Reader* (New York: McKay, 1977), p. 379.

38. They can be contacted at: www.westarinstitute.org.

Figure 19. Bruce Herman, *Bonhoeffer,* from the series *Elegy for Witness* (2001)

Figure 20. Richard C. Harden, *Nenad,* from the series *Faces of the Balkan War* (2002)

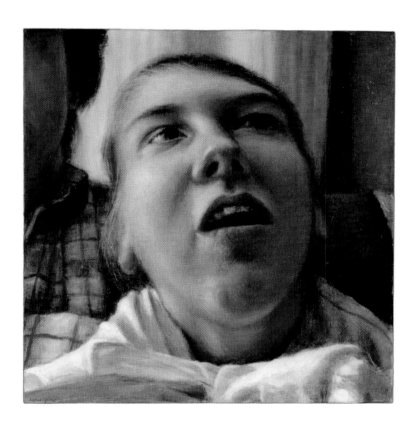

Figure 21. Timothy Grubbs Lowly, *In Ekstasis* (2001)

offered a kaleidoscope of Jesus identities: itinerant cynic philosopher, prophetic sage, "man of the spirit," eschatological prophet, radical social reformer, Jewish messiah, or a combination thereof.[39] The work of the Jesus Seminar inspired an upsurge of publishing on numerous aspects of Jesus' life and work, some defending traditional understandings of Jesus, others offering more radical interpretations. The resulting debate led to the notable PBS documentary series *From Jesus to Christ: The First Christians* (1998), which continues to be shown on public television. It was unique for the engaging way in which it introduced recent controversial New Testament scholarship to a general audience.

In the world of cinema, Quebec filmmaker and former Catholic altar boy Denys Arcand produced his remarkable contemporary allegory *Jesus of Montreal,* wherein a troupe of underemployed young actors attempt to update a moribund Passion Play for the city's cathedral, only to find that real life has seeped into the Gospel narrative. In the United States, New York director Martin Scorsese filmed Nikos Kazantzakis's searching novel *The Last Temptation of Christ,* which incorporated the author's imagined possibilities for a Jesus who counts the cost of his self-sacrifice. In 2002, *Joshua,* based on the popular novel wherein Jesus appears in the modern world, resulted in a limp noodle effort. More ambitiously, in 2003 a United Kingdom and Canadian team produced the three-hour *The Gospel of John,* which was rushed into theatres to take advantage of the controversy anticipating Mel Gibson's *The Passion of the Christ,* released on Ash Wednesday, 2004. Gibson's grueling account of Jesus' arrest, trial, crucifixion, death, and resurrection got embroiled in the culture wars because of its lengthy, graphic violence and because of fears of inciting anti-Semitism. No one — Christian or Jew, agnostic or atheist — was prepared for the

huge audience that flocked to this film, which recalls a nineteenth-century and premodern Catholic sensibility. It is fair to say that there has been no shortage of images of Jesus on television or movie screens in the last fifteen years.

Coinciding with the appearance of numerous books and films on Jesus, the year 2000 marked the end of the second millennium. In the West, the Gregorian calendar has been understood to date from the supposed birth of Christ in "year one." Under Christendom, that long period of history when Christianity held sway in the culture of Europe and the Americas, the citing of specific years within and after Jesus' lifetime was preceded by A.D., *anno domini,* "in the year of our Lord." Ongoing secularization has diminished this notion of the sacred marking the temporal.

Nevertheless, the millennial concept became a factor in the organization of two large and important art exhibitions — one in London, the other in Edmonton, Alberta, Canada — that were staged to consider the meaning of the long legacy of Jesus Christ in art and culture. The more ambitious of the two, *Seeing Salvation: Images of Christ in Art,* appeared at London's National Gallery and assembled a number of historically significant works from British public collections. It also spun off a BBC television series and two books.[40] Concurrent with the London exhibit, *Anno Domini: Jesus Through the Centuries — Exploring the Heart of Two Millennia* opened at the Provincial Museum in Alberta. Both exhibitions enjoyed unprecedented attendance from the secular curious and the faithful. Of the latter, many were infrequent or first-time museum-goers.

It is doubtful, however, that either of these projects would have happened if it weren't for the organizers' senior positions within their museums and the non-TAW vision of art and cultural history they held. At the National Gallery, director Neil MacGregor was a committed Anglican; at the Provincial

39. Ben Witherington III, *The Jesus Quest: The Third Quest for the Jew of Nazareth,* 2nd ed. (Downers Grove, IL: InterVarsity Press, 1997), is a synthesis from a traditional New Testament theological perspective. It straddles popular and scholarly approaches in its review and critique of recent Jesus scholarship at the end of the century.

40. Neil MacGregor with Erika Langmuir, *Seeing Salvation: Images of Christ in Art* (New Haven: Yale University Press, 2000); Gabriele Finaldi et al., *The Image of Christ* (London: National Gallery, 2000).

Museum, David Goa, Curator of Folklife, was a committed Roman Catholic.[41]

As a result of these "Jesus events" — publishing, films, museum exhibitions, and other similar enterprises — in secular culture, Jesus has enjoyed new and wide interest beyond the precincts of the church, established orthodoxies, or conventional piety. This is not to say, however, that any or all of these developments have made their way into TAW's realm or caught its notice. On the contrary, TAW remains oblivious or resistant to them. So when a number of contemporary artists joined the cultural production prompted by new interest in Jesus and began to engage him seriously in their art via theology, history, anthropology, or personal quests, TAW had no framework for evaluating their work, except skepticism, suspicion, or fear. Contemporary images of Jesus do not fit TAW's paradigm, which assumes, so to speak, that religion must decrease in order that secular (read "progressive") expressions may increase.

One of the artists in the *Broken Beauty* group, the painter Melissa Weinman, undertook a series of quirky depictions of saints in the 1990s that coincided with the reawakening of her religious sensibility.[42] Desiring a deeper understanding of her life, she sought counsel from an Anglican priest who was also a Jungian analyst. During her sessions with the priest, Weinman found that Jesus was a problematic figure for her, bound up in negative family dynamics, which made her reluctant to engage him in her spiritual life. The priest challenged her to draw Jesus in order to "find the Christ that you can trust completely." Weinman took up the quest and found her model for Jesus in a seminary student who worked part time as a carpenter. Despite its appearance, *Study for Christ: Matthew* (fig. 22) is not intended to evoke the crucifixion; rather, the subject suggested

to the artist a disciplined and physically strong man, stripped for action, as if capable of suspending himself from gymnastic rings. The work later caught the attention of Sr. Wendy Beckett, a juror for *Jesus 2000,* a competition sponsored by the *National Catholic Reporter* that was searching for artwork depicting Christ. Beckett said about *Study for Christ,* "Here is the powerful Son of Man, arms wide open to accept the Father's will."[43]

A similar composition — though purely archetypal — is used in David Robinson's relief sculpture in cement, *Cruciform Diptych* (fig. 23). The human form in the left wing is in positive relief; its companion figure is negative, recessed. Together they form a mold for a "Christ," the first human in God's act to redeem, "re-create," a new humanity in the image of Jesus. As such, the modest terracotta-toned work invokes the Incarnation, making it one of the few effective conceptual figurative sculptures in recent memory.

In *Font,* Robinson takes the cruciform in another direction (fig. 24). Now three-dimensional, his bronze of Jesus-as-Everyman is here more naturalistically modeled — though attenuated, gauntly elegant. His posture derives from traditional sculpted crucifixions: sagging body, head bowed, arms spread, one leg bent over the other. Robinson's clay construction of his figures (the form that is duplicated in bronze) gives them the appearance of being flayed or deeply scarified — fitting in *Font* — and calls to mind theologian Bruno Forte's notion of the crucifixion as Christ's self-abbreviation that becomes a form of beauty: "on the cross, Christ, the crucified God, is the place where beauty happens: in his self-emptying, eternity is present in time, the All who is God is present in the fragment of Christ's human form. It is the cross that reveals the beauty that saves."[44]

Robinson's Jesus, in addition to portraying the

41. David J. Goa et al., *Anno Domini: Jesus Through the Centuries — Exploring the Heart of Two Millennia,* two-volume exhibition catalog (Edmonton: The Provincial Museum of Alberta, 2000). Goa is also a scholar of Eastern Orthodox Christianity. In a conversation with Goa, he said that the exhibition took place despite considerable resistance from some of the Provincial Museum's staff.

42. Elizabeth Forst, "Lives of the Saints," *American Artist,* May 2000, pp. 44-49, 79-80.

43. "Jesus 2000," a supplement to the *National Catholic Reporter,* December 24, 1999, pp. 7, 17.

44. Bruno Forte, *The Essence of Christianity,* Italian Texts and Studies on Religion and Society, trans. P. David Glenday (Grand Rapids: Eerdmans, 2003), pp. 103-4. See his chapter, "Towards the Beauty of God," for an up-to-date Catholic theology of beauty.

crucifixion, takes on a second identity, that of a water-bearing coolie, among the lowest of physical laborers. The work retains the horizontal beam of the cross, and over the shoulders of Jesus it also becomes the burdensome means for delivering water, the liquid of life. As the water decants from the buckets, Jesus' elongated body appears poured out, too, breaking down under the weight. *Font* is also a functional fountain, and in this aspect it symbolizes Jesus' life and teaching as analogous to the "living water" that he will offer to the spiritually thirsty ("the water that I shall give will become a spring of water within, welling up for eternal life," John 4:14b). With its simultaneous images of the crucified Christ *and* the one who gives the living water of life, Robinson has advanced the iconographical tradition of Jesus.

Poured water is central to a pair of paintings entitled *The Baptism of Christ,* studies that John Nava did as part of his commission for the recently built Cathedral of Our Lady of the Angels in Los Angeles (fig. 25).[45] These studies were used to create the tapestry that hangs in the cathedral's baptistery, measuring over forty feet high. The paintings depict a semi-nude Jesus, his back to us, kneeling to receive a traditional baptism from the prophet John, who pours a bowl of water over the supplicant's head. We are struck by the power and beautiful masculine form evident in Nava's Jesus, so notable in the upper body. We are also aware that Christ is bowed — in effect, broken — in submission so that he will have his part in establishing God's saving justice for the community of believers that will follow after him.

Another work evoking "behold the man" is Jerome Witkin's iconic *Perfect and Me,* an oil painting from 1998 (fig. 26). The artist spent a number of years on various series and single pictures probing at the Jesus that had gotten under his skin. Some of these bordered on the blasphemous, others seemed to place Jesus in the history of anti-Semitism. *Perfect and Me* recalls that moment in the Gospels when

Jesus was taken prisoner prior to his crucifixion. The artist used a Jewish friend as a model for Christ; the "me" is the hand holding the gun, Witkin himself. In this regard Witkin participates in what Neil MacGregor reminds us was the difficult task facing artists who have portrayed Jesus for over two thousand years: "[In doing so] they explored the fundamental experiences of every human life. Pictures about Jesus' childhood, teachings, sufferings and death are — regardless of our beliefs — in a very real sense pictures about us."[46]

Kentucky painter Gaela Erwin's *Self-Portrait as Christ* (fig. 27) shows us a kind of Jesus from the tradition of imagery of "the Man of Sorrows."[47] In addition to this work, she has undertaken a series of probing self-portraits, empathically fusing her identity with an array of male and female saints. Erwin has a deep interest in the art of the late Renaissance and Baroque, and *Self-Portrait as Christ* is a Postmodern loop back into art history to create a mini-altarpiece for the present. A human heart appears in the predella below Erwin, who, as Christ, lifts her eyes painfully but resolutely into the light, as if taking in the Passion that lies before her on the journey to transcendence. It also seems to recall the moment from the Gospel of John when Jesus is presented by Pontius Pilate to the mob: "Jesus came out wearing the crown of thorns and the purple robe. Pilate said, 'Here is the man.' When they saw him, [they] shouted: 'Crucify him! Crucify him!'" (John 19:5-7a).

Ecce homo — behold the man: and through him, behold the ongoing mystery of the Incarnation. It is the mystery that never stops asking, Who *was* he? Who *is* he?

---

45. Information on Nava's work for the baptistry tapestries and the larger tapestry decorative program for the cathedral can be found at: www.olacathedral.org.

46. MacGregor with Langmuir, *Seeing Salvation,* p. 7. Witkin has recently found his spiritual identity in what he calls "a Jewish form of Christianity."

47. *Encounters: Gaela Erwin,* exhibition catalog (Huntsville: Huntsville Museum of Art, 2002).

Figure 22. Melissa Weinman, *Study for Christ: Matthew* (1998)

Figure 23. David Robinson, *Cruciform Diptych* (1999)

Figure 24. David Robinson, *Font* (2003)

Figure 25. John Nava, study for *Baptism of Christ* tapestry

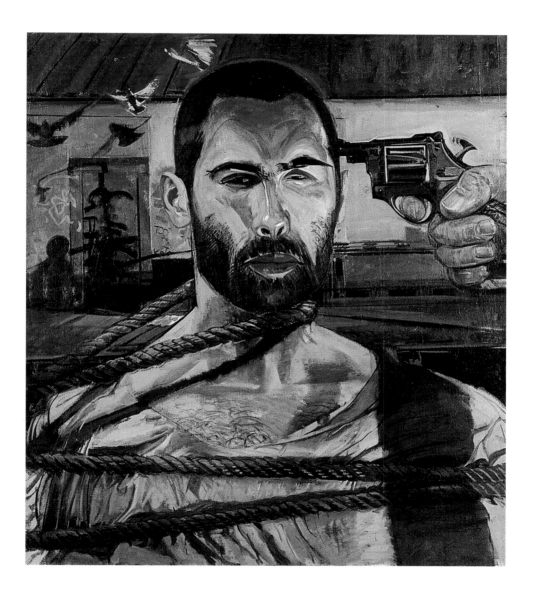

Figure 26. Jerome Witkin, *Perfect and Me* (1998)

Figure 27. Gaela Erwin, *Self-Portrait as Jesus* (2003)

EXHIBIT LOCATIONS

The *Broken Beauty* exhibit is appearing in the following locations:

LAGUNA ART MUSEUM
Laguna Beach, California
November 6, 2005, to February 26, 2006

JOSEPH D. CARRIER GALLERY
Columbus Centre, Toronto, Canada
April to May 2006

GABRIELLE BAKKER is a painter living and working in Seattle, Washington. She received her B.F.A. from the School of the Art Institute of Chicago and her M.F.A. from Yale University in New Haven, Connecticut. She has exhibited nationally, and her work is housed in a number of public collections.

LISA DEBOER received her B.A. in art history and German from Calvin College in Grand Rapids, Michigan, and her Ph.D. in the history of art from the University of Michigan. She is Assistant Professor of Art at Westmont College in Santa Barbara, California. Her primary area of research is early modern Netherlandish art, and she has published on print culture and historiography in the Netherlands between 1580 and 1648.

STEPHEN DE STAEBLER is a sculptor who lives and works in the San Francisco, California, area. He received his A.B. from Princeton University, Princeton, New Jersey, and his M.A. from the University of California, Berkeley, California. He has received a number of commissions and has exhibited nationally and internationally, and his work is housed in several public collections, including the Metropolitan Museum of Art, New York, New York.

GEALA ERWIN is a painter living and working in Louisville, Kentucky. She received her B.F.A. from the Columbus College of Art and Design, Columbus, Ohio, and her M.A. from the University of Louisville, Louisville, Kentucky. She also studied at the Studio Art School of the Aegean, Samos, Greece. She has exhibited nationally and internationally, and her work is housed in a number of public collections.

GORDON FUGLIE received his M.A. in art history from the University of California at Los Angeles. He is currently the Director of Laband Art Gallery at Loyola Marymount University in Los Angeles, California. He has also worked at the J. Paul Getty Museum in Malibu and the Grunwald Center for the Graphic Arts at the University of California at Los Angeles.

ERICA GRIMM-VANCE is a painter currently serving as Sessional Assistant Professor of Art and Visual Arts Coordinator at Trinity Western University, British Columbia, Canada. She received her B.F.A. Degree of Great Distinction from the University of Regina, Saskatchewan. She has exhibited in the United States and Canada, and her work is housed in numerous public collections, including the Vatican Collection, Vatican City, Italy.

RICHARD C. HARDEN, a painter, is Professor of Painting and Drawing at Manchester Community College, Manchester, Connecticut. He received his B.F.A. from the College of Visual and Performing Arts, Syracuse University, New York, and his M.F.A. from the Hartford Art School, University of Hartford, Connecticut. He has exhibited nationally and internationally, and his work is housed in numerous public collections, including the Metropolitan Museum of Art, New York, New York, and the Vatican Collection, Vatican City, Italy, and the National Gallery of Art, Tirana, Albania.

BRUCE HERMAN is a painter living and working in Gloucester, Massachusetts. He completed undergraduate and graduate fine arts degrees at Boston University School for the Arts. He is currently Professor of Art at Gordon College, in Wenham, Massachusetts, where he serves as Chairman of the Visual Arts and is Director of The Gallery at Barrington Center for the Arts. He has exhibited nationally and internationally. His work is housed in many private and public collections, including the Vatican Museum of Modern Religious Art in Rome.

EDWARD KNIPPERS is a painter who works out of a studio in Manassas Park, Virginia. He received his B.A. from Asbury College, Wilmore, Kentucky, and his M.F.A. in painting from the University of Tennessee, Knoxville, Tennessee. He has exhibited his work widely in the United States and internationally.

TIMOTHY GRUBBS LOWLY is a painter who has served as instructor and artist-in-residence at North Park University, Chicago, Illinois, and as Director of Exhibitions at the Carlson Tower Gallery, North Park University, Chicago, Illinois. He received his B.F.A. from Calvin College, Grand Rapids, Michigan. He has exhibited nationally and internationally, and his work is housed in many public collections, including the Metropolitan Museum of Art, New York, New York.

MARY McCLEARY is a painter. She was Regent's Professor of Art at the Stephen F. Austin State University, Nacogdoches, Texas. She received her B.F.A., cum laude, from Texas Christian University, Fort Worth, Texas, and her M.F.A. from the University of Oklahoma, Norman, Oklahoma. She has exhibited nationally, and her work is housed in a number of public collections.

JOHN NAVA is a painter and tapestry designer. He lives and works in Ojai, California, northwest of Los Angeles. He received his B.A. from the College of Creative Studies, University of California, Santa Barbara, and his M.F.A. from Villa Schifanoia, Graduate School of Fine Art, Florence, Italy. He has received many commissions, nationally and internationally, and has exhibited in the United States. His commissioned tapestries for the Cathedral of Our Lady of Angels in Los Angeles were the winner of the 2003 National Interfaith Forum on Religion, Art and Architecture Design Honor Award for Visual Art.

THEODORE PRESCOTT is a sculptor who received his B.A. degree from The Colorado College and his M.F.A. degree from the Maryland Institute College of Art. He is a Distinguished Professor of Art at Messiah College in Grantham, Pennsylvania, and is past president of Christians in the Visual Arts. His work is housed in several private and public collections, including the Vatican Museum of Modern Religious Art in Rome.

DAVID J. ROBINSON is a sculptor who works and teaches from studios in Vancouver, British Columbia. He studied in the fine arts program at Vancouver Community College and in the sculpture program at Ontario College of Art in Toronto, Canada. His work is housed in a number of public collections, and he has exhibited widely, particularly in Canada.

JOEL C. SHEESLEY, a painter, is Professor of Art at Wheaton College, Wheaton, Illinois. He received his B.F.A. from Syracuse University in Syracuse, New York, and his M.F.A. from Denver University in Denver, Colorado. He has exhibited nationally and internationally.

TIMOTHY VERDON is a Roman Catholic priest and art historian. He received his Ph.D. from Yale University, and he is a fellow of the Harvard University Center for Italian Renaissance Studies in Florence, Vila i Tatto. He is a Canon of the Florence Cathedral and Director of the Archdiocesan Office for Catechesis through Art, as well as a member of the Board of Directors of the Cathedral Museum. He also teaches for Stanford University in Florence and for the Facoltaga Teologica dell'Italia Centrale. His recent publications include books on sacred art in Italy, on Mary in European art, on sacred space, and on the Vatican complex.

MELISSA WEINMAN, a painter, is Professor of Art at the University of Puget Sound, Tacoma, Washington. She received her A.B. from Bowdoin College, Brunswick, Maine, and her M.F.A. from the University of Southern California, Los Angeles, California. Her work is housed in several public collections, and she has exhibited nationally and internationally.

PATTY WICKMAN, a painter, is Professor and Vice Chair in the Department of Art at the University of California, Los Angeles, California. She received her B.F.A. from Arizona State University, Tempe, Arizona, and her M.F.A. from the University of Colorado, Boulder, Colorado. She has exhibited nationally and internationally.

JEROME WITKIN is a painter; he is currently Professor in the Studio Arts Department at Syracuse University, Syracuse, New York. He received his undergraduate degree from the Cooper Union School of Art, New York, New York, and his M.F.A. from the University of Pennsylvania, Philadelphia, Pennsylvania. His work has been exhibited widely in the United States.

Foreword

Figure 1. Philip Guston, *Conspirators*, ca. 1930 (originally painted as part of WPA Artist Project). Oil on canvas, 50 × 36 inches. Painting destroyed by vandals. Courtesy of the McKee Gallery, New York.

Figure 2. Philip Guston, *The Studio*, ca. 1969. Oil on canvas, 48 × 42 inches. Private collection. Courtesy of the McKee Gallery, New York.

Chapter 1, "The Bodies Before Us"

Figure 1. Alberto Giacometti, *Man Pointing*, 1947. Bronze, 70.5 inches high. Gift of Mrs. John D. Rockefeller III. The Museum of Modern Art, New York. © 2004 Artists Rights Society (ARS), New York/ADAGP, Paris. Photo credit: Digital Image © The Museum of Modern Art/Licensed by Scala/Art Resource, NY.

Figure 2. Pablo Picasso, *Les Demoiselles d'Avignon*, 1907. Oil on canvas, 96 × 92 inches. The Museum of Modern Art, New York. Acquired through the Lille P. Bliss Bequest. © 2004 Estate of Pablo Picasso/ Artists Rights Society (ARS), New York. Photo credit: Digital Image © The Museum of Modern Art/Licensed by Scala/Art Resource, NY.

Figure 3. Howard Finster, *The Way of Jesus*, 1982. Enamel on wood. Lehigh University Art Galleries Museum Operation, Zoellner Arts Center, Bethlehem, Pennsylvania.

Figure 4. Philip Pearlstein, *Two Female Models in Bamboo Chairs with Mirror,* 1981. Oil on canvas, 72³⁄₁₆ × 72⅛ inches. The Toledo Museum of Art, purchased with funds from the Libbey Endowment, Gift of Edward Drummond Libbey, 1982.121 © TMA 1982.

Figure 5. Cindy Sherman, *Untitled Film Still #7,* 1978. Black and white photograph, 8 × 10 inches. Courtesy of the artist and Metro Pictures.

Figure 6. Cindy Sherman, *Untitled #137,* 1984. Color photograph, 70.5 × 47.75 inches. Eli and Edythe L. Broad Collection, Los Angeles. Courtesy of the artist and Metro Pictures.

Figure 7. Leon Golub, *Interrogations II,* 1980-81. Acrylic on canvas, 304.8 × 426.7 cm. Gift of The Society for Contemporary Art 1983.264. Reproduction, The Art Institute of Chicago. © Leon Golub/Licensed by VAGA, New York, NY. Courtesy of Ronald Feldman Fine Arts.

Figure 8. Barbara Kruger, *Untitled (Your gaze hits the side of my face),* 1981. Photograph, 55 × 41 inches. Courtesy: Mary Boone Gallery, New York. Photo credit: Zindman/Fremont.

Figure 9. Leon Golub, *Reclining Youth,* 1959. Lacquer on canvas, 78¾ × 163½ inches (200 × 415.3 cm). Collection Museum of Contemporary Art, Chicago, Susan and Lewis Manilow Collection of Chicago Artists. © Leon Golub/Licensed by VAGA, New York, NY. Courtesy of Ronald Feldman Fine Arts. Photograph © Museum of Contemporary Art, Chicago.

Figure 10. "System Lymphatica," whole body specimen showing the lymphatic vessels, in Museo di Storia Naturale dell Università di firenze, sezione di Zoologia La Specola, pages 409-10 in *Encyclopedia Anatomica.*

Figure 11. Kiki Smith, *Untitled (A Man),* 1988. Ink on gampi paper, 121.9 × 96.5 × 17.8 cm. Gift of the Lannan Foundation, 1997.121. Photograph by Susan Einstein. Reproduction, The Art Institute of Chicago.

Figure 12. Kiki Smith, *Virgin Mary,* 1992. Wax with pigment on cheesecloth and wood on steel base, 67½ × 26 × 14½ inches (171.5 × 66 × 36.8 cm). Collection of the artist. Courtesy of Pace Wildenstein. Photograph by Ellen Page Wilson.

Figure 13. Edward Schmidt, *Oreads,* 2000. Oil on canvas, 42 × 84 inches. Hacket-Freedman Gallery, San Francisco.

Chapter 2, "Broken Beauty, Shattered Heart"

Figure 1. Edvard Munch, *The Scream,* 1893. Oil on canvas. National Gallery, Oslo, Norway. © 2004 The Munch Museum/The Munch-Ellingsen Group/Artists Rights Society (ARS), New York. Photo credit: Erich Lessing/Art Resource, NY.

Figure 2. *Jesus and the Multiplication of the Loaves and Fishes,* sixth century. Mosaic, Sant'Apollinare Nuovo, Ravenna, Italy. Photo credit: Erich Lessing/Art Resource, NY.

Figure 3. Anonymous Aretine Master, *Painted Cross with St. Francis,* ca. 1260: detail. San Francesco, Arezzo, Italy. Photo credit: Scala/Art Resource, NY.

Figure 4. Nicola Pisano, pulpit, 1260: detail. Baptistery, Pisa, Italy. Photo credit: Scala/Art Resource, NY.

Figure 5. Nicola Pisano, pulpit, 1265-67: detail, Christ on cross. Cathedral, Siena, Italy. Photo credit: Scala/Art Resource, NY.

Figure 6. Giotto, *Crucifixion,* ca. 1305. S. Maria Novella, Florence, Italy. Photo credit: Scala/Art Resource, NY.

Figure 7. Filippino Lippi, *Madonna and Child,* ca. 1445. Palazzo Medici Riccardi, Florence, Italy. Photo credit: Scala/Art Resource, NY.

Figure 8. Piero della Francesca, *Baptism of Christ,* ca. 1450. National Gallery, London. Photo credit: Erich Lessing/Art Resource, NY.

Figure 9. Detail of Francesca's *Baptism of Christ:* the face of Christ. Photo credit: Erich Lessing/Art Resource, NY.

Figure 10. Gianlorenzo Bernini, *Cardinal Scipione Borghese,* ca. 1632. Drawing, red chalk over graphite, on paper, 9¹⁵⁄₁₆ × 7¼ inches. The Pierpont Morgan Library, New York City, New York. Photo credit: The Pierpont Morgan Library/Art Resource, NY.

Figure 11. Nicolas Poussin, *Landscape with Saint John on Patmos,* 1640. Oil on canvas, 100.3 × 136.4 cm. A. A. Munger Collection, 1930.500. Reproduction, The Art Institute of Chicago.

Figure 12. Caspar David Friedrich, *The Wayfarer,* 1818. Oil on canvas, 94.8 × 74.8 cm. Kunsthalle, Hamburg, Germany. Photo: Elke Walford. Photo credit: Bildarchiv Preussischer/Art Resource, NY.

Figure 13. Eugène Delacroix, *The Death of Sardanapalus,* 1827. Oil on canvas, 392 × 496 cm. Louvre, Paris. Photo: Hervé Lewandowski. Photo credit: Réunion des Musées Nationaux/Art Resource, NY.

Figure 14. Edgar Dégas, *The Absinthe Drinker,* 1876. Musée d'Orsay, Paris, France. Photo: Hervé Lewandowski. Photo credit: Réunion des Musées Nationaux/Art Resource, NY.

Figure 15. Gustave Moreau, *Apparition of St. John the Baptist's Head to Salome,* 1876. Musée de Moreau, Paris. Photo: J. G. Berizzi. Photo credit: Réunion des Musées Nationaux/Art Resource, NY.

Figure 16. Paul Gaugin, *The Vision After the Sermon,* 1888. National Gallery of Scotland, Edinburgh. Scotland. Photo credit: Art Resource, NY.

Figure 17. Emile Nolde, *Dance Around the Golden Calf,* 1910. Neue Pinakothek, Munich, Germany. Courtesy of The Nolde-Museum. Photo credit: Erich Lessing/Art Resource, NY.

Figure 18. Pablo Picasso, *Head of a Woman,* 1909. Bronze, 16¼ × 10⅜ × 10¾ inches (41.27 × 26.35 × 27.30 cm). Albright-Knox Art Gallery, Buffalo, New York, Edmund Hayes Fund, 1948. © 2004 Estate of Pablo Picasso/Artists Rights Society (ARS), New York.

Figure 19. Georg Grosz, *Metropolis,* 1916-17. Thyssen-Bornmisza Collection, Madrid. © Estate of George Grosz/Licensed by VAGA, New York, NY. Photo credit: Bridgeman Art Library International.

Figure 20. Georg Grosz, *Manikin Without a Face or Hands,* 1920. Kunstsammlung Nordrhein Westfallen, *Dusseldorf.* © Estate of George Grosz/Licensed by VAGA, New York, NY. Photo credit: Bridgeman Art Library International.

Figure 21. Roy Lichtenstein, *Drowning Girl,* 1963. Oil and synthetic polymer paint on canvas, 67⅝ × 6¾ inches. The Museum of Modern Art, New York. Philip Johnson Fund and Gift of Mr. and Mrs. Bagley Wright. Photo credit: Digital Image © The Museum of Modern Art/Licensed by Scala/Art Resource, NY.

Chapter 3, "A Comic Vision? Northern Renaissance Art and the Human Figure"

Figure 1. Michelangelo, *Creation of Adam,* 1508-1512. Fresco. Sistine Chapel, Vatican. Photo credit: Scala/Art Resource, NY.

Figure 2. Michelangelo, *The Drunkenness of Noah,* 1508-1512. Fresco. Sistine Chapel, Vatican. Photo credit: Scala/Art Resource, NY.

Figure 3. Michelangelo, *God Separating Light from Darkness,* 1508-1512. Fresco. Sistine Chapel, Vatican. Photo credit: Scala/Art Resource, NY.

Figure 4. Hubert and Jan van Eyck, Ghent Altarpiece, 1432. Oil on panel. Cathedral of St. Bavo, Ghent. Photo credit: Scala/Art Resource, NY.

Figure 5. Hubert and Jan van Eyck, *The Adoration of the Lamb,* detail from the Ghent Altarpiece. Cathedral of St. Bavo, Ghent, Belgium. Photo credit: Scala/Art Resource, NY.

Figure 6. Albrecht Altdorfer, *The Battle of Issus,* 1529. Oil on panel, 52.25 × 47.25 inches. Alte Pinakothek, Munich, Germany. Photo credit: Scala/Art Resource, NY.

Figure 7. Pieter Bruegel the Elder, *The Harvesters,* ca. 1565. Oil on panel, 46.5 × 63.25 inches. Metropolitan Museum of Art, New York, Rogers Fund, 1919 (19.164). Photograph © The Metropolitan Museum of Art.

Figure 8. Hieronymus Bosch, *Seven Deadly Sins and Four Last Things,* ca. 1480-1490. Oil on panel. Museo del Prado, Madrid, Spain. Photo credit: Erich Lessing/Art Resource, NY.

Figure 9. Pieter Bruegel the Elder, *The Wedding Feast,* ca. 1566. Oil on panel, 45 × 64 inches. Kunsthistorisches Museum, Vienna, Austria. Photo credit: Erich Lessing/Art Resource, NY.

Figure 10. Pieter Bruegel the Elder, *The Wedding Dance,* ca. 1566. Oil on panel, 47 × 62 inches. Detroit Institute of Art, Detroit.

Figure 11. Jan Steen, *The Happy Company (As the Old Sing, So Pipe the Young),* ca. 1665. Oil on canvas, 52.75 × 64.25 inches. The Mauritshuis, The Hague. Photo credit: Scala/Art Resource, NY.

Figure 12. Jan Steen, *Marriage at Cana,* 1676. Oil on canvas, 31⅜ × 43 inches. The Norton Simon Foundation, Pasadena, California.

Figure 13. Pieter Bruegel the Elder, *The Way to Calvary,* ca. 1564. Oil on panel, 48.75 × 67 inches. Kunsthistorisches Museum, Vienna, Austria. Photo credit: Erich Lessing/Art Resource, NY.

Figure 14. Hieronymus Bosch, *Christ Mocked (The Crowning with Thorns),* ca. 1479 or later. Oil on panel, 29 × 23 inches. © The National Gallery, London.

Figure 15. Duane Hanson, *Tourists,* 1970. Polychromed fiberglass and polyester, 64 × 65 × 47 inches each. The Scottish National Gallery of Modern Art. Art © Estate of Duane Hanson/Licensed by VAGA, New York, NY.

Mary McCleary, *I fled him down the days and down the nights,* 2000. Mixed media collage on paper, 45 × 70½ inches. Courtesy of the artist and of the Art Museum of Southeast Texas, Beaumont, Texas.

Chapter 4, "Beauty Lost, Beauty Found: One Hundred Years of Attitudes"

Figure 1. Alphonse Mucha, *Nature,* ca. 1900. Gilt bronze, silver, marble, 27¼ H × 11 W × 12 inches D (69.2 × 27.9 × 30.5 cm). Virginia Museum of Fine Arts, Richmond. The Sydney and Frances Lewis Art Nouveau Fund. Photo credit: Katherine Wetzel. © Virginia Museum of Fine Arts.

Figure 2. Marcel Duchamp, *Nude Descending a Staircase, #2,* 1912. Oil on canvas, 57⅞ × 35⅛ inches. Collection of the Philadelphia Museum of Art. The Louise and Walter Arensberg Collection, 1950. © 2004 Artists Rights Society (ARS), New York/ADAGP, Paris/Succession Marcel Duchamp. Photo credit: The Philadelphia Museum of Art/Art Resource, NY.

Figure 3a. Janine Antoni, *Lick and Lather,* 1993. Seven soap and seven chocolate self-portrait busts, each bust 24 × 16 × 13 inches. Installation View: Hirshhorn Museum. Courtesy of the artist and Luhring Augustine. Photo credit: Lee Stalsworth.

Figure 3b. Detail, single chocolate head, from Janine Antoni, *Lick and Lather.* Photo credit: John Bessler.

Figure 4. Michael Kenna, *Tre Colline Vineyard, Napa Valley, California, USA,* 2003. Photograph. Courtesy of the artist.

Figure 5. Freeman Patterson, *Light in the Forest,* 1995. Courtesy of the artist.

Figure 6. Peter Voulkos, *USA 41,* 1960. Stoneware, epoxy paints, slips, light glaze, 19¾ × 11¾ × 10½ inches. Gift of Wayne Parrish. Collection of the Corcoran Gallery of Art, Washington, DC.

Figure 7a. Michelangelo, View of the Ceiling of the Sistine Chapel, Vatican City, Rome, 1508-1512. Fresco, 118 × 42 feet. Photo credit: Art Resource, NY.

Figure 7b. Michelangelo, *The Delphic Sibyl,* from the Ceiling of the Sistine Chapel, Vatican City, Rome, 1508-1512. Fresco, approximately 108″ high. Photo credit: Scala/Art Resource, NY.

Figure 8. Umberto Boccioni, *The City Rises,* 1910. Oil on canvas, 78.5 × 118.5 inches. Mrs. Simon Guggenheim Fund. Collection of the Museum of Modern Art, New York. Photo credit: Digital Image © The Museum of Modern Art/Licensed by Scala/Art Resource, NY.

Figure 9. Georges Rouault, "Nous sommes foux" (We are mad), pl. 39, *Miserere et Guerre,* ca. 1920 (published 1948). Aquatint. © 2004 Artists Rights Society (ARS), New York/ADAGP, Paris. Photo credit: Bridgeman Art Library International.

Figure 10. John Currin, *The Pink Tree,* 1999. Oil on linen, 78¹/₁₆ × 48¹/₁₆ inches. Hirshhorn Museum and Sculpture Garden, Smithsonian Institution, Joseph H. Hirshhorn Purchase Fund, 2000. Photo credit: Lee Stalsworth.

Figure 11. Ken Price, *Ornette,* 2003. Ceramic, acrylic, 21½ × 21 × 15½ inches. Courtesy of Franklin Parrasch Gallery, Inc. Photo credit: Michael Korol.

Chapter 5, *"A Broken Beauty* and Its Artists"

Figure 1. Gabrielle Bakker, *Eve and Her Conscience,* 1998. Egg tempera and oil on two panels, 12 × 20 inches each. Courtesy of the artist.

Figure 2. Edward Knippers, *The Harvest (Adam and Eve),* 2002. Oil on panel, 96 × 144 inches. From the collection of Howard and Roberta Ahmanson.

Figure 3. Joel Sheesley, *Nakedness on the Journey,* 1997. Oil on canvas, 50 × 70 inches. Courtesy of the artist.

Figure 4. Joel Sheesley, *After Paradise,* 2002. Oil on canvas, 72 × 79 inches. Courtesy of the artist.

Figure 5. Mary McCleary, *Children of the Apple Tree,* 2000. Mixed media collage on paper, 44.5 × 74 inches. Collection of Kathy and Bud Wright.

Figure 6. Bruce Herman, *Annunciation,* from the series *Elegy for Witness,* 2002. Oil and alkyd resin, gold and silver leaf on panel, 81 × 106 inches. Collection of Mr. and Mrs. William R. Cross, Manchester, Massachusetts.

Figure 7. Patty Wickman, *Overshadowed,* 2001. Oil on canvas, 78 × 104 × 2 inches. Courtesy of the artist.

Figure 8. Melissa Weinman, *Schutzmantelmadonna,* 1996-1997. Oil on canvas (triptych), 74 × 156 inches. Courtesy of the artist.

Figure 9. Jerome Witkin, *Entering Darkness,* 2001. Six panels. Oil on canvas. Panel 1: 67 × 76 inches. Panel 2: 72 × 42 inches. Panel 3: 75 × 30 inches. Panel 4: 77 × 59 inches. Panel 5: 109 × 104 inches. Panel 6: 130 × 76 inches. Courtesy of the artist and Jack Rutberg Fine Arts, Los Angeles.

Figure 10. Richard C. Harden, *My Breath,* flanked by two panels, both entitled *Falling,* 2001. Oil on panel, polyptych installation. *My Breath,* 90 × 229 inches (3 panels); *Falling,* 90 × 48 inches each. Courtesy of the artist and the National Gallery of Art, Tirana, Albania.

Figure 11. Stephen De Staebler, *Yoke-Winged Man,* 1994. Bronze, 92.25 × 46.5 × 40 inches. Collection of Russ Solomon.

Figure 12. Erica Grimm-Vance, *Swimming in Existence: The Cloud of Unknowing,* 1999-2001. Steel, encaustic, and gold leaf, 35 × 45 inches. Courtesy of the artist.

Figure 13. Erica Grimm-Vance, *With Great Effort We Remembered,* 2002. Steel, encaustic on birch, 45 × 30 inches. Collection of Thomas S. Woods and Lydia M. Lovison.

Figure 14. David Robinson, *On Holy Ground,* 1999. Bronze and steel, 12 × 14 × 14 inches. Courtesy of the artist.

Figure 15a. Timothy Grubbs Lowly, *Carry Me,* 2002. Drawing on toned panel, 108 × 48 inches. Collection of Andreas Waldburg-Wolfegg.

Figure 15b. Detail, from Timothy Grubbs Lowly, *Carry Me.*

Figure 16. Patty Wickman, *Anonymous (with St. Agatha),* 1996. Oil on canvas, 78 × 55 inches. Collection of Tricia and Ken Volk.

Figure 17. Melissa Weinman, *St. Agatha's Grief,* 1996. Oil on canvas, 42 × 42 inches. Courtesy of the artist.

Figure 18. Jerome Witkin, *Between a Ladder and Smoke: Edith Stein,* 1997. Oil on canvas, 25 × 29 inches. Collection of Maryanne Mott and Herman Warsh.

Figure 19. Bruce Herman, *Bonhoeffer,* from the series *Elegy for Witness,* 2001. Alkyd resin on wood panel, gold and silver leaf, 76 × 48 inches. Collection of Messiah College, Grantham, Pennsylvania.

Figure 20. Richard C. Harden, *Nenad,* from the series *Faces of the Balkan War,* 2002. Giclee print, Arches paper, 45 × 34 inches. Courtesy of the artist.

Figure 21. Timothy Grubbs Lowly, *In Ekstasis,* 2001. Acrylic on panel, 12.5 × 12 inches. Courtesy of the artist.

Figure 22. Melissa Weinman, *Study for Christ: Matthew,* 1998. Charcoal and conté crayon on paper, 40 × 27.5 inches. Collection of the Seattle University School of Law.

Figure 23. David Robinson, *Cruciform Diptych,* 1999. Cement, 10¾ × 16½ inches each panel. Courtesy of the artist.

Figure 24. David Robinson, *Font,* edition 9, 2003. Bronze, copper, and steel, 62 × 47 × 47 inches. Courtesy of the artist.

Figure 25. John Nava, Study for *Baptism of Christ* tapestry. Oil on canvas, 48 × 48 inches. © 2003 John Nava/The Cathedral of Our Lady of The Angeles. Used by permission.

Figure 26. Jerome Witkin, *Perfect and Me,* 1998. Oil on canvas, 44.25 × 38.25 inches. Collection of Dr. Jeremy Jackson.

Figure 27. Gaela Erwin, *Self-Portrait as Jesus,* 2003. Oil on two panels, 22 × 14.5 inches each panel. Collection of Ms. Jean Distler.

INDEX